M

C000000344

THE
MINISTRY

Addresses to Students
of Divinity

CHARLES J. BROWN

THE BANNER OF TRUTH TRUST

THE BANNER OF TRUTH TRUST
3 Murrayfield Road, Edinburgh EH12 6EL, UK
P.O. Box 621, Carlisle, PA 17013, USA

© The Banner of Truth Trust 2006

ISBN-10: 0 85151 931 8
ISBN-13: 978 0 85151 931 9

Typeset in 11/15 pt Sabon at
the Banner of Truth Trust
Printed in the U.S.A. by
Versa Press, Inc.,
East Peoria, IL

CONTENTS

BIOGRAPHICAL
INTRODUCTION

Charles John Brown, the youngest of the five sons of Alexander Brown, was born on 21 August 1806. His father ran a bookselling business in Aberdeen and was twice Provost of that city. Charles grew up closest to the fourth son, David, and both brothers became assured of a saving relationship to Christ during student days in Edinburgh, in the 1820s, where they sat under the ministry of Dr Robert Gordon.

It was his conversion that ended Charles Brown's preparation to be a lawyer and set him on the course that led to his being elected minister of Anderston Church of Scotland, Glasgow, in 1831. Six years later, in 1837, he became minister of the New North Church in Edinburgh. Almost his entire congregation removed to the Free Church of Scotland at the Disruption of 1843, and they ultimately settled in the building on Forrest Road that remains today. He was minister of this charge until his death in 1884, and it was said of him, 'Never had any minister a more attached or united congregation; and they have been a highly favoured one.'[1]

His brother David, who also left the Church of Scotland for the Free Church, was to be more widely remembered by later generations on account of his work as an author and the gifts that led to his becoming Principal of the Free Church College in Aberdeen. But C. J. Brown gave his life to the one great purpose of preaching and pastoring, and in that capacity he was the equal of the most eminent men of his day. Unlike his brother, he has had no biographer, but W. G. Blaikie, in comparing the brothers in his *Life of David Brown*, said that Charles 'was decidedly ahead of him in preaching gifts and spiritual power'.[2] In another place, when listing 'Men of Mark' in the Free Church, Blaikie characterized the younger Brown as, 'An animated, incisive, and very spiritual preacher.'[3]

At the Disruption of 1843, ministers and elders of the Free Church first gathered in the Tanfield Hall,

---

[1] *Disruption Worthies: A Memorial of 1843* (Edinburgh: Greig, 1876) p. 71.

[2] W. G. Blaikie, *David Brown* (London: Hodder and Stoughton, 1898), p. 11.

[3] W. G. Blaikie, *After Fifty Years . . . the Jubilee of the Free Church of Scotland in 1893* (London: Nelson), p. 138.

Edinburgh, and it was in that building, the following Sunday afternoon, that C. J. Brown was called upon to preach to three thousand. His text was, 'I have set watchmen upon thy walls, O Jerusalem; which shall never hold their peace, day nor night.'

With the inevitable controversy that accompanied the events surrounding the Disruption there was a concern among the Free Church leaders that the priority of personal devotion to Christ could be displaced. For that reason, in the following year, the General Assembly of May 1844 was preceded by a day of humiliation and prayer and for the first meeting of the day, prior to discussion, Charles Brown was asked to preach. He took for his theme the minister's responsibility and aim, on the basis of the words, 'I will stand upon my watch, and set me upon my tower, and will watch to see what he will say unto me, and what I shall answer when I am reproved' (*Hab.* 2:1).

The message of that Tuesday in May 1844 was long to be remembered. Brown began by reminding his hearers that the purpose of their meeting was 'not so much to speak to one another as to speak to the Lord our God, and pour out our hearts before him in sorrowful confession of our many, many short comings and sins'; and this in order that it might 'please Him in infinite mercy to make some use of us as His instruments in the great work on which His heart is set, and for which the Son of God died'.

He went on: 'How is a minister to teach others the ways of God unless he is walking close and straight in them himself? How shall he lay open the sins of others, not harshly but tenderly, unless he is seeing and mourning in secret over his own.' Eight lines of thought were then taken up, before he concluded with the verses of Isaiah 6 – 'Woe is me, for I am undone' – then the live coal taken from off the altar, the iniquity taken away, and the words, 'Whom shall I send, and who will go for us? Then said I, Here am I: send me.'

Before the sermon concluded we read that, 'Many a head was bowed, and here and there amidst the Assembly men were silently seeking relief in tears.'[1] The discussion that was expected did not follow. Instead, after a few words by Dr Chalmers, there was silence: 'In vain the Moderator invited further

---

[1] Thomas Brown, *Annals of the Disruption,* new edition (Edinburgh: MacNiven, 1892), p. 630. Brown gives a full description of the sermon and its effect. Horatius Bonar agrees with Thomas Brown on the effects of 'Dr C. Brown's admirable sermon' but whereas the author of *Annals* dated it May 21, Bonar gave the date as May 17, 1844. *Life of John Milne of Perth* (London: Nisbet, 1868), p.107.

discussion. Men's hearts were full; the Assembly remained for a time in hushed silence. It seemed as if members were afraid to disturb the solemnity of the scene; as if it would be best for each to retire and enter into his closet, and shut the door behind him. At a quarter past two o'clock the blessing was pronounced, and men went to their homes.'

It is only from such fragments as this that we gain a glimpse of the man who was made a D.D. by Princeton in 1863. Of his participation in the Kilsyth revival of 1839, his congregation's evangelistic outreach into the Cowgate area of Edinburgh, his occasional printed addresses,[1] and his support for Moody in 1874, of all these and much else we know little. His only books were *The Divine Glory of Christ* (1868)[2] and *The Way of Life* (1874), both of which were made up of sermons.

These are valuable books although they cannot, as one who heard him comments, 'give a full idea of his liveliness and warmth in the pulpit'. The same

[1] These included his sermon of 21 May 1843; *The Disruption Question Stated* (repr. with additions, Edinburgh: Nelson, 1863); *The General Assembly's Call to Prayer* (Edinburgh: Maclaren, 1869); and *The Ensuing Assembly: Letter of Dr Charles J.Brown to Dr Horatius Bonar* (Edinburgh: Greig, 1873). A sermon on Genesis 3:24, The Expulsion from Eden, is included in the present volume as an example of his preaching.

[2] New edition, Edinburgh: Banner of Truth, 1982.

writer says of his opening prayer on Sunday morn-
ings:

> We have heard it said of it by more than one,
> that they could have gone home with the feel-
> ing that they had received spiritual strength from
> it for many days, so full was it of true devot-
> ional spirit and communion with God . . . In his
> lectures and sermons there was a rare combin-
> ation of intellectual power and spiritual
> earnestness, proceeding from a mind and heart
> full of the treasure of the Word. Truly the Word
> of Christ dwelt in him richly in all wisdom, so
> that alike in the pulpit and at the Communion
> Table, at his prayer meetings, in his classes, in
> family visitation, and at the sick-bed, he fed his
> people with what had first enriched his own
> soul.[1]

The work here reprinted survives as a statement
of what he saw as the essence of the gospel ministry.
Had these lessons been remembered the state of Scotland would be far different from what it is today,
where one may see what was once the New North
Church on Forrest Road converted into the 'Bedlam
Theatre'.

[1] 'Charles John Brown' in *Disruption Worthies*, p. 67.

Brown would remind us that there is such a thing as preaching with the Holy Spirit sent down from heaven. Christ can give such men again: men of doctrinal earnestness, catholic spirit, tender hearts, and abiding prayerfulness. Such messengers, touched with a 'live coal from off the altar', have ever been the means of resurrection and revival within the churches. And only then can the church be the means of awakening the world that sleeps.

There is one particular hindrance to such a revival and Charles Brown often spoke of it. He noted how, in periods when spiritual conditions are low, love and forbearance grow weak while disputes and controversies among Christians become common.

When, in his words, 'There is little communion with God, little striving against sin, little pressing after the divine image,' then, 'Disputes and discords rush in to fill up the very vacuum.' He continued:

I am quite well aware that, in existing circumstances, many controversies must be continued; but let the church only be revived – let a spirit of faith and holiness be but extensively poured forth – and the circumstances will change; and we shall find far too much to do setting ourselves against the common enemy, to have either leisure or heart for contentions among our-selves.[1]

Much similar wisdom will be found in the pages now in the reader's hands. Only let the Christian ministry return to the apostolic rule of Acts 6:4 and the churches will surely see brighter days.

IAIN H. MURRAY
Edinburgh,
May 2006

---

[1] 'Symptoms and Fruits of a Revival of Religion,' in *Lectures on the Revival of Religion by Ministers of the Church of Scotland* (Glasgow, Collins, n.d. [*c.*1840]; repr. Edinburgh: Banner of Truth, 1984), p. 325. This lesson was evidently exemplified in his own congregation. We read; 'The spiritual temperature of the members and office-bearers being kept high, there was no jarring or jealousy.' *Disruption Worthies*, p. 71.

AUTHOR'S PREFACE

The following Addresses to Students of Divinity were delivered at different periods within the last ten years, and have been widely circulated in their separate form. A desire has often been expressed for the issuing of them together, and in a shape somewhat more permanent. In complying with the wish – only adding the largest part of my closing Address to the Free Church General Assembly – I desire humbly to commend the little Manual to the blessing of the adorable Head of the church.

A distinguished minister, writing to me two years ago respecting the Addresses to Students, suggested the enlarging of them into a small treatise on the whole subject of the pastorate. After weighing the suggestion, however, I came to the conclusion that, besides other difficulties in the way, I should thus lose the simplicity, the freedom and directness of address, and of course the brevity, to which is very much owing, I am persuaded, whatever acceptance these Addresses have found with ministers and students. In revising them, accordingly, I have made very little change, beyond removing, here and there, what in the new shape would have been needless repetition – although I fear the reader will still find more of this than I could have wished, or could easily avoid without an entire change of structure.

CHARLES J. BROWN
Edinburgh,
November, 1872

I

THE CONNECTION BETWEEN GODLINESS AND THE CHRISTIAN MINISTRY

I address you this evening at the request of a Committee of Presbytery, appointed in connection with an overture before that Court of which the following are the opening words: 'It is humbly overtured that the General Assembly shall seriously consider whether some more special examination ought not to be made before young men enter the Divinity Hall, but especially before they receive licence, in regard to their personal profession of religion.'

Thus I have thought it might be suitable and useful, by the blessing of the Lord, if I should select for the subject of my address *the connection between personal godliness and the Christian ministry.*

The subject is a very sacred, deeply solemn and searching, one; and I desire, and must ask leave of you, and of my brethren here, in dealing with it to use all possible simplicity and plainness of speech.

For distinctness' sake, I will lay down two positions; and, after some illustration of them, I will offer a few more immediately practical hints or suggestions. *First,* conversion to God, personal godliness, is the foundation, and an indispensable prerequisite, of the Christian ministry. *Second,* during the whole course of the ministry, after it has been entered on, there continues to subsist the most intimate mutual connection between godliness and the ministry, – a powerful reciprocal influence of each upon the other.

1. *Conversion to God, personal godliness, is the foundation, and an indispensable prerequisite, of the Christian ministry.* Now I should be ashamed to go into any formal proof of this, as of a thing that could be disputed. Nobody here can possibly question it. The beginnings, at least, of personal godliness are necessary even to sitting down warrantably at the table of the Lord, much more to entering into the *ministry* of the Lord.

But though not in the way of proving a thing disputed, yet in order to the impressing on my own mind and yours of a thing unspeakably important, I will attempt to illustrate the position a little from two different sources – from the nature, distinctive ends, strength necessary for, and grand instrument of, the ministry; and then from several texts of the Word of God.

i. As to the *nature* of the ministry, it is, as the word indicates, *a service* of and from the Lord Jesus, about the highest spiritual things of his kingdom. Well; the position is already established, so far as mere proof is necessary. For, an unconverted man, a man destitute of personal godliness, is an *enemy* to Christ. 'The carnal mind is enmity against God; it is not subject to the law of God, neither indeed can be' (*Rom* 8:7). To imagine that Jesus should commission an enemy for any such service is out of the question. The ministry is a high and very confidential service of the Lord Jesus. It is an ambassador's service of a sovereign who employs him to negotiate peace with his enemies; it is the service rendered to a bridegroom by a friend whom he employs to assist about his espousals. It is an ambassador's service of a sovereign. 'We are ambassadors for Christ, as though God did beseech you by us: we pray you in Christ's stead, be ye reconciled to God' (2 *Cor.* 5:20). What sovereign would think of employing one of his enemies to negotiate peace with the rest?

It is the service rendered to a bridegroom by a friend whom he employs to assist about his marriage. Said John the Baptist, 'He that hath the bride is the bridegroom: but the friend of the bridegroom, which standeth and heareth him, rejoiceth greatly because of the bridegroom's voice; this my joy therefore is fulfilled' (*John* 3:29). I suppose, indeed, that the 'friend of the bridegroom' here means an *official* friend. But the official friendship presupposes the personal. Bridegrooms are not wont to ask strangers, much less enemies, to be helpful about their espousals.

Then, as to the distinctive *ends* of the ministry, here they are in two words – 'I send thee to the Gentiles, to open their eyes, to turn them from darkness to light, and from the power of Satan unto God, that they may receive forgiveness of sins, and inheritance among them which are sanctified by faith that is in me' (*Acts* 26:18); *and*, 'for the work of the ministry, for the edifying of the body of Christ' – 'whom we preach, warning every man and teaching every man in all wisdom, that we may present every man perfect in Christ Jesus' (*Eph.* 4:12; *Col.* 1:28). But to both ends an unconverted man is an utter stranger. He knows nothing of them. He cannot seek, aim at, prosecute, either of them.

The *strength* again, necessary for the ministry, – for the discharge of its duties and the attaining of its ends, is none other than the Holy Ghost. 'Who is sufficient for these things? Our sufficiency is of God'

(2 *Cor.* 2:16; 2 *Cor.* 3:5). 'No man can say that Jesus is the Lord, but by the Holy Ghost' (*1 Cor.* 12:3). The unconverted man 'has not the Spirit of Christ' – he is 'none of his' (*Rom.* 8:9). He is a stranger at once to the whole strength, and to the prayers which bring it down.

Lastly, the *instrument* of the ministry is the Holy Scripture. It is enough here to remind you of the solemn words, 'The natural man receiveth not the things of the Spirit of God; for they are foolishness unto him: neither can he know them, because they are spiritually discerned' (*1 Cor.* 2:14).

ii. But now passing, for illustration of our position, to some weighty texts of Scripture, turn, first, to Galatians 1:15–16: 'It pleased God, who separated me from my mother's womb, and called me by his grace, to reveal his Son in me, *that I might preach him*' (ινα ευαγγελιζωμαι αυτον). Paul tells us that God had done two things for him, in order that he might preach Christ. He had called him by his grace; and, more specifically, had revealed Christ in him. He had called him from death to life, – out of darkness into his marvellous light. God would not have a man still in darkness, in death, to preach the living, life-giving Redeemer, even had the thing been possible, which it was not. Paul could not preach a Saviour he did not know. And thus, more specifically, God had revealed his Son in him. The expression sends us back to such words as those, 'Whom say ye that I am? And Simon Peter answered and said, Thou art the Christ, the Son of the living God. Jesus answered and said unto him, Blessed art thou, Simon Bar-jona; for flesh and blood hath not revealed it unto thee, but my Father which is in heaven' (*Matt.* 16:15–17).

Again, turn to John 21:15: 'So when they had dined, Jesus saith to Simon Peter, Simon, son of Jonas, lovest thou me more than these? He saith unto him, yea, Lord: thou knowest that I love thee. He saith unto him, Feed my lambs.' A terrible doubt had been cast over the entire religion of Peter, and he had virtually separated himself from the society of the apostles, by his denials of Jesus in the high priest's palace. In order to his restoration to that work which before had been committed to him, – 'thou shalt catch men', – the doubt required to be as openly removed as it had been openly created. No stranger to the love of the glorious Shepherd might or could 'feed his lambs'. 'Lovest thou me? Yea, Lord; thou knowest that I love thee. Jesus saith unto him, Feed my lambs. He saith to him again the second time, Simon, son of Jonas, lovest thou me? He saith unto him, Yea, Lord; thou knowest that I love thee. He saith unto him, Feed my sheep' (21:16). Wholly out of the question that a *wolf* (and what else are *we* if we belong not to Jesus?) should be set to feed the sheep! 'He saith unto him the third time, Simon, son of Jonas, lovest thou me? Peter was grieved because he said unto him the third time, Lovest thou me? And he said unto him, Lord, thou knowest all things; thou knowest that I love thee. Jesus saith unto him, Feed my sheep' (21: 17).

I would just add before leaving this great passage, that if indeed the Lord Jesus shall say to *you*, 'Feed my sheep, feed my lambs', then shall you, amid the trials and manifold difficulties of your work, have this blessed support, that when, on a Saturday evening for example, you might be ready to sink beneath the weight of the duties of the next day, you shall be able, in the spirit of Moses at Horeb, to plead, 'See, thou sayest unto me, Bring up this people: and thou hast not let me know whom thou wilt send with me. Yet thou hast said, I know thee by name, and thou hast also found grace in my sight. Now therefore, I pray thee, if I have found grace in thy sight, shew me now thy way, that I may know thee, that I may find grace in thy sight: and consider that this nation is thy people' (*Exod.* 33:12–13). And to you also the Lord shall say, 'My presence shall go with thee, and I will give thee rest' (verse 14). Ay, and your deepest Sabbath joys shall not rarely follow close on your heaviest Saturday trials.

Again, turn to Paul's words in 2 Corinthians 5:18, 20: 'All things are of God, who hath reconciled us to himself by Jesus Christ, and hath given to us the ministry of reconciliation . . . Now then we are ambassadors for Christ, as though God did beseech you by us: we pray you in Christ's stead, be ye reconciled to God.' He hath *reconciled us to himself, and hath given to us the ministry of reconciliation.* For, as observed near the beginning, sovereigns employ not enemies about their negotiations of peace. Yet here is a marvellous thing – an enemy *reconciled,* a man *once* an enemy entrusted with the ministry of reconciliation!

Oh, none so fit for such a ministry – fitter than an angel, now, the man who, having been reconciled, knows both the blessedness of the peace and the terribleness of the war, – who can plead with the enemies in the lowly and tender spirit of those words, 'I am the least of the apostles, that am not meet to be called an apostle, because I persecuted the church of God. But by the grace of God I am what I am' (*1 Cor.* 15:9–10). 'This is a faithful saying, and worthy of all acceptation, that Christ Jesus came into the world to save sinners, of whom I am chief' (*1 Tim.* 1:15).

The only other passage I would ask you to turn to is 1 Timothy 1:12: 'I thank Christ Jesus our Lord, who hath enabled me, for that he counted me faithful, putting me into the ministry' – first intimating, that Christ would not (yea, to speak with reverence, could not) 'enable' him for such a ministry, being still faithless; and further, expressly declaring that Christ first counted him faithful, and then put him into the ministry. With which let 2 Timothy 2:2 be compared, 'The things that thou hast heard of me among many witnesses, the same commit thou to faithful men, who shall be able to teach others also' – as if to say, that only faithful men shall ever be able to teach (ικανοι διδαξαι) the faith to others.

Without asking you to turn to them, I remind you of such further great words as the following – 'Unto me, who am less than the least of all saints, is this grace given, that I should preach among the Gentiles the unsearchable riches of Christ' (*Eph.* 3:8). Again (*1 John* 1:1, 3), 'That which was from the beginning, which we have heard, which we have seen with our eyes, which we have looked upon, and our hands have handled, of the Word of Life; . . . that which we have seen and heard declare we unto you, that ye also may have fellowship with us: and truly our fellowship is with the Father, and with his Son, Jesus Christ.' Again (2 *Cor.* 4:5–7), 'We preach not ourselves, but Christ Jesus the Lord; and ourselves your servants for Jesus' sake. *For* God, who commanded the light to shine out of darkness, hath shined in our hearts, to give the light of the knowledge of the glory of God in the face of Jesus Christ. But we have this treasure in earthen vessels' – Oh yes, earthen vessels, but no longer 'vessels of wrath', – *earthen* vessels, frail, ready to fall to pieces, yet 'vessels of mercy', – 'vessels unto honour, sanctified, and meet for the Master's use, prepared unto every good work.'

At your leisure you might do well also to study the principles – the whole analogy – of the consecration of Aaron and his sons to the priesthood, in Leviticus, eighth chapter. Thus, at the 22nd verse, 'Moses brought the other ram, the ram of consecration: and Aaron and his sons laid their hands upon the head of the ram. And he slew it; and Moses took of the blood of it; and put it upon the tip of Aaron's right ear, and upon the thumb of his right hand, and upon the great toe of his right foot. And he brought Aaron's sons, and Moses put of the blood upon the tip of their right ear, and upon the thumbs of their right hands, and upon the great toes of their right feet.' Compare that whole glorious passage in Isaiah 6:5–9, 'Then said I, Woe is me! for I am undone; because I am a man of unclean lips, and I dwell in the midst of a people of unclean lips: for mine eyes have seen the King, the Lord of hosts. Then flew one of the seraphim unto me, having a live coal in his hand, which he had taken with the tongs from off the altar: and he laid it upon my mouth, and said, Lo, this hath touched thy lips; and thine iniquity is taken away, and thy sin purged. Also I heard the voice of the LORD, saying, Whom shall I send, and who will go for us? Then said I, Here am I; send me.'

Personal godliness, in short, is the foundation, and an indispensable prerequisite, of the Christian ministry. It is the *foundation* of it. I venture to affirm that it is three parts of the ministry out of four. No doubt, there *is* a fourth part which is quite necessary. But so prominent and pre-eminent, is the godliness, that I think an unlettered peasant, with the love of Christ burning in his heart, were fitter for the ministry than the most learned of men 'dead in trespasses and sins'!

2. Our second position is, that *during the whole course of the ministry, after it has been entered on, there continues to subsist the closest mutual*

connection between the two elements – the strongest reciprocal influence of godliness on the ministry, and of the ministry on godliness.

i.   *Of godliness on the ministry.* Take two views of this rapidly. (1.) All the subject-matters of the ministry might be reduced to two – *Sin*, and *Christ*. Sin. But he alone can tell of sin, to much purpose, whose inmost soul is touched with the sense of his own sin. Oh, it is a horrible thing to hear men talk coldly, indifferently, or, which is much the same, harshly, vociferously, of sin and wrath and hell. It can but pain and shock the serious, and tend to harden the careless and impenitent. He only is fit to deal with such themes who, with a spirit chastened and subdued, is entering in some measure into the soul of those words, 'Woe is me! for I am undone' – 'I abhor myself, and repent in dust and ashes' – 'Sinners, of whom I am chief' – 'The good that I would I do not, and the evil that I would not, that I do' (*Isa.* 6:5; *Job* 42:6; *1 Tim.* 1:15; *Rom.* 7:19).

And then, Christ. He only shall tell to much purpose of the glorious Saviour who is fain to break forth, 'Thou art fairer than the sons of men' – 'My beloved is white and ruddy, the chiefest among ten thousand' – 'Tell me, O thou whom my soul loveth, where thou feedest, where thou makest thy flock to rest at noon; for why should I be as one that turneth aside by the flocks of thy companions?' – 'Set me as a seal upon thine heart, as a seal upon thine arm; for love is strong as death, jealousy is cruel as the grave' – 'The love of Christ constraineth us' (*Psa.* 45:2; *Song of Sol.* 5:10; 1:7; 8:6; 2 *Cor.* 5:14).

Let me ask you to turn here with me to a single passage in Paul's Second Epistle to Timothy – an epistle which might be named Paul's divine charge to that young minister, penned, as I think it doubtless was, during his second imprisonment at Rome, and when, no longer simply bound to a soldier in his own hired lodging, but immured in Nero's dungeon, he was soon to be brought forth to martyrdom. Says he, 'Whereunto I am appointed a preacher, and an apostle, and a teacher of the Gentiles. For the which cause I also suffer these things: nevertheless *I am not ashamed;* FOR I know whom I have believed, and am persuaded that he is able to keep that which I have committed unto him against that day' (1:11-12). So it seems that the grand secret of all Paul's sufferings and services for the Lord Jesus, lay just in one grand, overwhelming service the Saviour had done for *him* – even that, when he, a miserable sinner, was ready to perish, Jesus had laid hold of him, and snatched him from the burning, and still was keeping his never-dying soul as a precious deposit committed to him, against the great day – 'for the which cause I also suffer these things: nevertheless I am not ashamed; *for* I know whom I have believed, and am persuaded that he is able to keep that which I have committed unto him against that day.'

(2.) Then take another view of the influence of godliness on the ministry. Reference was made near the outset to the *strength* for the ministry, the Holy Ghost; and to the great *instrument* of it, the Scriptures. But as for the strength, the man whose soul is prosperous before the Lord is one living at the very fountainhead of that strength – drawing supplies of it, by ceaseless prayer, for the finding of suitable subjects and themes from week to week; for the obtaining of all necessary materials in connection with the themes; for the whole meditating of the things concerning the King and his kingdom; for the delivering of them with the needed skill, and tenderness, and power; for passing from household to household of the people; for the visiting of the sick and dying – for the whole work and duty of the ministry together.

And as to the *instrument*, the Scriptures, are they not, to such a minister, the 'man of his counsel', his 'songs in the house of his pilgrimage', 'more precious than thousands of gold and silver', 'sweeter than honey from the honeycomb'? (*Psa.* 119:54; 119:72; 19:10). Can he fail thus to grow daily more at home, as it were, in the use of his *weapon*, the sword of the Spirit, which is the Word of God?

ii. But there remains to be touched on the influence of the ministry reciprocally on the personal godliness. And here I desire, for myself, to give humble thanks to the Lord that ever he gave me a *profession* which goes hand in hand with the soul's everlasting blessedness – where the work and the everlasting welfare run in parallel, yea rather, ever converging, lines. For I hold it to be nothing else than a libel on the ministry to charge it with a tendency to render a minister's piety coldly professional and intellectual. A poor piety, methinks, that can be so rendered!

No doubt there *is* such a thing as an unholy familiarity with the things and themes of the Scripture – a dreadful rock to dash against, truly, where the profession and the piety run not in parallel, but in divergent lines. But blessed be God, there is, if we are but true to ourselves and our work, a *holy* familiarity also with the things and themes of the Scripture – the sacred volume becoming more and more a minister's bosom companion and friend. Again I say, I desire to give solemn thanks for a profession in which the better a man by grace is, the better he shall do his work; and the better he does his work, still the better a man he shall become, and the more ready, when the work is done, 'to depart, and be with Christ' (*Phil.* 1:23), which for him, at least, shall be best of all!

But now, in conclusion, I venture to offer a few more immediately practical hints or suggestions. Of course, the entire subject raises the question for every student, and for *me*, Am I indeed Christ's? Have I been called effectually out of darkness into God's marvellous light? Know I that conversion, that personal godliness, which is the foundation, and an indispensable prerequisite, of the ministry. Have I indeed known what the Catechism has from childhood taught me – 'Effectual calling is the work of God's Spirit, whereby, convincing us of our sin and misery, enlightening our minds in the knowledge of Christ, and renewing our wills, he doth persuade and enable us to embrace Jesus Christ, freely offered to us in the gospel?'

The question might have three different answers. First, a distinctly negative one. In that case, what ought to be done? Suppose I address any for whom the negative answer is the only true one, is their right course to flee out of the Divinity Hall straightway? I believe that there is another, and 'more excellent way'. Oh, take heed lest thus you should turn your backs, at one and the same time, on the ministry and on heaven. God gives you no liberty to *remain* strangers to his grace, to continue without his Christ even for another day. To perish is a crime; to be without the Saviour is a crime. 'This is his commandment, that we believe on the name of his Son Jesus Christ' (*1 John* 3:23). Therefore, at once to his feet! 'Awake thou that sleepest, and arise from the dead, and Christ shall give thee light' (*Eph.* 5:14). Listen to the voice, 'I am the resurrection and the life; he that believeth in me, though he were dead, yet shall he live.'

With Bartimaeus by the wayside, cry, 'Jesus, thou Son of David, have mercy upon me' (*Luke* 18:38). And if the multitude rebuke thee to hold thy peace, cry the more. Soon shall Jesus say to thee also, 'What wilt thou that I should do unto thee?' (18:40). And thou shalt answer, 'Lord, that mine eyes may be opened' (*Matt.* 20:33). And Jesus shall have compassion on thee, and touch thine eyes, and thou shalt receive sight, and follow him in the way. Not a few have entered the Divinity Hall out of Christ, who, brought to him in the course of their studies, have left it, by his sovereign grace, burning with his love – chosen vessels to bear his name to sinners all around.

Or the question may have an answer neither decisively negative nor affirmative, but of painful doubt and hesitation. In such a case I would say, first, that a man's doubting of his conversion by no means proves him unconverted; though, if he can be content to live on in his doubts, and take them easy, this, indeed, would go far to prove him Christless. But, secondly, if even ascertained non-conversion demand not the abandonment of the ministry straightway, far less can mere doubts of it, however grave. And therefore your course is, to carry these doubts straight to Jesus – to beseech him to resolve them. Or, better still, carry your whole case and misery together to him. Throwing yourself at his feet, plead on his naked word, 'Him that cometh to me I will in no wise cast out' (*John* 6:37). Cry, 'Lord, save me, I perish – Lord, to whom shall I go? (*Matt.* 8:25; *John* 6:68). Entreat me not to leave thee, nor to return from following after thee – I will not let thee go, except thou bless me' (*Ruth* 1:16; *Gen.* 32:26).

But the third answer the question may receive is the happily and hopefully affirmative one. In this case, let me say, first more generally, seek, throughout the entire course of your divinity studies, to 'keep your heart with all diligence' (*Prov.* 4:23). Take heed to *yourselves* (*1 Tim.* 4:16). Flee youthful lusts and follow after righteousness, godliness, faith, love, patience, meekness (2 *Tim.* 2:22). More specifically, may I offer these hints?

1. Have some reading always of a more personal and experimental character, besides that which is more strictly professional. I remind you of such books as Owen's *Indwelling Sin*, or *Spiritual-mindedness*, or *Temptation*; or, Howe's *Delighting in God*; or, Guthrie's *Trial of a Saving Interest*; or, Baxter's *Saints' Rest*; or Rutherford's *Letters*. Of these last, by the way, there happen to be just about as many as there are days of the year, and they would form delightful daily portions for reading. You will find the edition with the notes of Mr Bonar of Glasgow a choice one.[1]

2. Be much in secret prayer, especially in the morning of each day. Guard against the temptation of running away from your knees to study, because you seem to get little comfort or good from your devotions. I may venture, in connection with this, to mention an incident in my own poor history. Soon after I entered the Aberdeen Divinity Hall, finding the first discoveries of the glorious gospel, which had broken on me some time before, to have lost a good deal of their first freshness and power, I was much

[1] Available from the present publisher (ISBN 0 85151 388 3).

tempted to hurry over secret morning prayer, and get to my studies, the former seeming to come to little profit. One day I happened to get into conversation with one very near and dear to me, who strongly advised perseverance amid difficulty, for a somewhat longer time, in the exercise of prayer, even though little comfort and little profit might seem to come of it. It proved to be a life-lesson. Nor has the fruit of it, I think, been ever since altogether lost.

3. Prize your Sabbaths, as the miser his gold, for converse with God, eternity, heaven. Give your Sabbaths wholly to these ends, excepting so much as you may occupy in seeking the welfare of others. And thus –

4. Have some work of a missionary character, among old or young, or both, during the entire course of your Hall studies. The prosperity, however, of your College Missionary Association assures me that I do not need to enlarge on this.

5. Dwell ever among the green pastures of the Word of God. Make it indeed your bosom companion. Feed on the Scriptures till they come to be incorporated with your spiritual being. Not only pray *and* read, but pray reading, with your Bible open before you, gazing into its exceeding great and

precious things, waiting till you apprehend them, or rather, till they *apprehend you* – literally 'getting them by heart' (as our expressive phrase is) longing to say with David, 'I rejoice at thy word as one that findeth great spoil', and with Jeremiah, 'Thy words were found, and I did eat them; and they were unto me the joy and rejoicing of my heart' (*Psa.* 119:162; *Jer.* 15:16).

I cannot close without congratulating you on the prospect of entering into the ministry in a time of un-wonted blessing – when the Lord is evidently making bare his arm, and saving many precious souls, wait-ing still to be gracious. What encouragement is there in such a time! But what responsibility also! Some are jealous of our *lay* brethren doing and saying so much for the salvation of souls. I for one can have no sym-pathy with the feeling. If the addressing by the lay brethren is liable to some abuse, the best way to meet the danger is for the Ministry, in place of keeping coldly aloof, to step in lovingly to superintend and direct. Of this I am thoroughly persuaded, both that those la-bours of our brethren are fitted to stimulate us to rise to a higher manner of preaching and of ministration; and that, if we are but true to ourselves, they shall raise the ministry to a place of higher esteem, impor-tance, power, than it has ever held in our day.

I have done. The Lord give you understanding in all things, and in due time say to you, 'Feed my sheep, Feed my lambs' – 'Come after me, and I will make you to become fishers of men' – 'Fear not, from henceforth thou shalt catch men!' (*John* 21:15-16; *Matt.* 4:19; *Luke* 5:10).

2

PUBLIC PRAYER

It is often alleged by Episcopalians – thrown out sometimes as a taunt against us – that we are too much a *preaching* church. I dissent wholly from the opinion. I believe that if our preaching is what it ought to be, we cannot be too much a preaching church, nor give too earnest attention to the whole subject of the preaching of the Word. Undoubtedly, however, we may be too little a *praying* church; or, to express it as in distinctive reference to my subject of today, we may *give too little attention to the devotional part of our public Sabbath services*. I am persuaded that we *do* give far too little attention to it.

Do not misunderstand me, however. It is not that we occupy too small a portion of time in the public prayers. It has long been my firm belief that a great evil among us – and this is the first thing to which I have to ask your attention – is the undue prolonging of the different prayers of the sanctuary, and, more particularly, the first, the opening, prayer of the service. Gentlemen, you are not likely to spend too much time in *secret* prayer. Perhaps there might be such a thing. But so rare is the evil among us, that I suppose there is no need of offering cautions on this head. But in social and public prayer, we may easily continue too long in prayer, – or in the words and attitude of prayer, at least; and I may as well at once state my humble but deliberate judgment to be, that about ten minutes is, ordinarily speaking, the limit to which any one public prayer should be prolonged; and I am persuaded that great and manifold evils come out of the exceeding of some such limit, frequently, or in ordinary circumstances. Let, me crave your attention to four distinct evils connected with it.

1. First and most obvious is *the evil of wearying out even the devout worshipper, both in body and spirit.* And I pray you to remember that when weariness begins, devotion ends; and further, that when devotion ends – the language and attitude of prayer being still continued – sin can scarce fail to begin, or, at the best, much sinful infirmity. For myself I can only say that over and over again I have been obliged to give up all attempts to accompany the minister in prayer, and just throw myself on the pity of him who 'knoweth our frame, and remembereth that we are dust' (*Psa.* 103:14). Of course the evil is

not a little aggravated by our practice of *standing* at prayer - although that posture is in accordance both with Scripture and the most ancient ecclesiastical usage. Our Episcopalian friends are, many of them, I believe, dissatisfied with the length of their own forenoon prayer-service. Undoubtedly, however, the evil of undue length is a less serious one when the words are lying in a book under the eye of the worshipper.

2. Then a second evil is, that *prayers thus unduly prolonged become, almost invariably, to a great extent preachings, or, at best, a kind of devout meditatings.* But prayer is neither preaching nor meditating, but the transacting of a great and urgent business with the living God. See at your leisure, for illustration, any of the leading examples of prayer recorded in Scripture for our use and imitation. Oh, it is a most painful thing to listen to recitals of nearly a system of theology in public prayer. And only less painful are those pious meditatings, where there is continuously poured out the language of a certain vague contemplating of the divine perfections and ways.

3. A third evil is *the placing of the whole after-part of the service at an immense disadvantage.* Even

the devout part of the audience, having been worn out at the beginning, hear the sermon, however good, with a certain restless impatience. True, some men excel so much in public prayer, that the hearer is but little wearied even though the exercise is very unduly prolonged. And there *are* preachers who, by the unusual power and eloquence of their discourses, even after long prayers overcome every disadvantage, and secure attention to the end. But these are exceptional cases. Far more generally the disadvantage of the long opening prayer is never overcome, and the whole after service is heavy and uninteresting.

4. But yet a fourth evil. *Our admirable method of extempore prayer is scandalized, and exposed to very plausible objections that would otherwise have no weight whatever.* I much more than approve, I rejoice in, our free, extempore prayer, and would shrink from being tied down to any liturgy, whether composed three centuries ago, or written by some minister of later days.

But if the question were put as between a really good liturgy, on the one hand, and those prayers wearisomely spun out to which one has sometimes to listen, on the other, I confess I should not find it very easy to defend our method. I must repeat my humble but deliberate conviction that ten minutes is the limit to which any one public prayer ought ordinarily to be prolonged.

And if any one is disposed to ask how it is possible to embrace all the usual topics of prayer in that time, I simply answer, Why seek to embrace them all in one prayer? What is the use of it? Ten minutes will be found fully sufficient for all that is desirable to be embraced in even the principal prayer of the service, provided those minutes are devoutly and wisely used – used according to the principles which now I would venture, in the second place, to suggest.

Let me, before leaving the matter of undue length, draw your attention to the following words from Livingstone's notice of Robert Bruce, of Edinburgh, the famous contemporary of Andrew Melville: 'No man in his time spoke with such evidence and power of the Spirit. No man had so many seals of conversion; yea, many of his hearers thought no man, since the apostles, spake with such power. . . . He was very short in prayer when others were present, but every sentence was like a strong bolt shot up to heaven. I have heard him say that he wearied when others were too long in prayer; but, being alone, he spent much time in wrestling and prayer.'

ii. But now, in the second place, I believe that one great *source* of the undue length of our public prayers lies in the inadequate measure of attention given among us to the whole subject, and, more specifically, the want of due forethought, premeditation, before the pulpit has been entered. Let me not be misunderstood. I am no advocate for the writing out of prayers and committing them to memory, and should greatly deprecate such a method. It is, however, a mere vulgar and groundless notion that there is no medium between this and a minister's entering his pulpit wholly at sea as to the prayers he is to offer. It is but a fancy that *free* prayer is all one with wholly *unpremeditated* prayer. Assuredly, the Westminster divines entertained no such opinion; for if you examine the *Directory for Public Worship* you shall find that, while they give no forms of prayer, they give very full materials after the tenor of which the minister is to pray.

What I plead for, and would press very earnestly, is the marking out in the mind of some leading line of thought and petition not to tie the minister down, but rather to set him more free. Only think what the case is: a pastor leading the devotions of the same people twice every Sabbath, from week to week - during a long course of years, it may be. In the absence of serious forethought it is almost impossible but that one of two results should follow; either he must slide gradually into a form of his own, a repetition substantially of the same things Sabbath after Sabbath (to which, would not a good liturgy be preferable?) or else, in trying to avoid this, he must wander up and down, as some ship at sea without compass or rudder, at the mercy of every wind that blows. There is one blessed wind, at least, he shall be little likely thus to catch, even the gales longed for in those words of the Song of Solomon, 'Awake, O north wind; and come, thou south; blow upon my garden, that the spices thereof may flow out' (*Song of Sol.* 4:16). Oh, I think if these gales are to be found, the soul must be free, the whole exercise must be spontaneous and unconstrained.

And observe that, though you may have marked out a certain line of thought and petition in your mind, you are nowise tied down to follow it, but may vary it endlessly, according as circumstances, under the adorable Spirit of grace, may suggest. It may only be added here that I include in forethought all earnest desires after a frame of spirit suitable for public prayer, before entering the pulpit. *The whole subject, in short, must come to occupy a larger place in our attention and esteem.*

It is here our Episcopalian friends are right regarding us. We do not give too much attention to preaching, but we give too little attention to the subject of our public prayers.

iii. But, thirdly, it has long appeared to my mind a great evil that a certain *cant phraseology,* or *stock of phrases,* has come somehow to be handed about from parish to parish, yea, down from generation to generation, until our good people have learned to regard it as all from the Bible, not only adopting it into their family and social prayers, but fathering it upon God's Word. Here, however, detail is everything; and I will give some examples of the phraseology referred to, arranging it, for the sake of distinctness, under two or three heads.

1. There is what might be called an unhappy, sometimes quite grotesque, mingling of Scripture texts. Who is not familiar with the following words addressed to God in prayer, 'Thou art the high and lofty One that inhabiteth eternity, *and the praises thereof*', which is but a jumble of two texts, each glorious taken by itself, but both marred, and one altogether lost, indeed, when thus combined and mingled. The one is Isaiah 57:15, 'Thus saith the high and lofty One, *that inhabiteth eternity,* whose name is Holy.'

The other is Psalm 22:3, 'Thou art holy, O thou that *inhabitest the praises of Israel.*' The inhabiting of the praises of eternity, to say the least, is meagre; there were no praises in the past eternity to inhabit. But what a glory is there in God's condescending to inhabit, take up his very abode in, the praises of Israel, of the ransomed church?

Then there is an example nothing less than grotesque under this head, and yet one in such frequent use that I suspect it is very generally regarded as having the sanction of Scripture. Here it is, 'We would put our hand on our mouth, and our mouth in the dust, and cry out, Unclean, unclean; God be merciful to us sinners.' This is no fewer than four texts joined, each beautiful by itself. First, Job 40:4, 'Behold I am vile; what shall I answer thee? I will lay my hand upon my mouth.' Second, Lamentations 3:29, 'He putteth his mouth in the dust; if so be there may be hope.' Third, Leviticus 13:45, where the leper is directed to put a covering upon his upper lip, and to cry, Unclean, unclean. And fourth, the publican's prayer. But how incongruous a man's first putting his hand on his mouth, then putting his mouth in the dust, and, last of all, crying out, etc.!

The only other example I give under this head is an expression nearly universal among us, and, I suspect, almost universally thought to be in Scripture, 'In thy favour is life, and thy loving-kindness is better than life.' The fact is, that this also is just an unhappy combination of two passages, in which the term *life* is used in altogether different, and even incompatible, senses, namely Psalm 30:5, 'In his favour is life', life, of course, in the higher sense of true blessedness; and Psalm 63:3, 'Thy loving-kindness is better than life', where, evidently, life means the present temporal life.

2. A second class may be described as unhappy alterations of Scripture language. Need I say that the 130th Psalm, 'Out of the depths', etc., is one of the most precious in the whole book of the Psalms? Why must we have the words of David and of the Holy Ghost thus given in public prayer, and so constantly that our pious people come all to adopt it into their social and family prayers, 'There is forgiveness with thee, that thou mayest be feared, and plenteous redemption *that thou mayest be sought after*' or 'unto'? How precious the simple words as they stand in the Psalm, (verse 4), 'There is forgiveness with thee, that thou mayest be feared' (verses 7–8); 'With the LORD there is mercy, and with him is plenteous redemption; and he shall redeem Israel

from all his iniquities'! Again, in this blessed Psalm, the words of the third verse, 'If thou, LORD, shouldest mark iniquities, O Lord, who shall stand?' too seldom are left us in their naked simplicity, but must undergo the following change, 'If thou wert strict to mark iniquity', etc. I remember in my old college days, we used to have it in a worse shape, 'If thou wert strict to mark or rigorous to punish!'

Another favourite change is the following:

'Thou art in heaven, and we upon the earth; therefore let our words be few *and well ordered.*' Solomon's simple and sublime utterance (full of instruction, surely, on the whole theme I am dealing with) is, 'God is in heaven, and thou upon earth; therefore let thy words be few' (*Eccles.* 5:2). For another example under this class, see how Habakkuk's sublime words are tortured, 'Thou art of purer eyes than to behold evil, and canst not look on sin *without abhorrence.*' The words of the Holy Ghost are (*Hab.* 1:13), 'Thou art of purer eyes than to behold evil, and canst not look on iniquity.' Need I say that the power of the figure, 'canst not look on iniquity', is nearly lost when you add that God *can* look on it, only not without abhorrence? Again, one sometimes hears the Book of Job thus quoted in prayer, 'Thou chargest thine angels with *comparative* folly!'

3. A third class is made up of meaningless pleonasms, vulgar commonplace redundancies of expression, in quoting from the Scriptures.

One of these has become so universal that I venture to say you seldom miss it when the passage referred to comes up at all. 'Be in the midst of us', (or, as some prefer to express it, somewhat unfortunately, as I think, 'in our midst') 'to bless us, and *to do us good.*' What additional idea is there in the last expression, 'and to do us good?' The passage referred to is Exodus 20:24, 'In all places where I record my name, I will come unto you, and I will bless you.' Such is the simplicity of Scripture. Our addition is, 'bless us and do us good'. In Daniel 4:35, we read the noble words, 'None can stay his hand, or say unto him, What doest thou?' The favourite change is, 'None can stay thy hand *from working.*' Again, 'Eye hath not seen, nor ear heard, neither have entered into the heart of man the things which God hath prepared for them that love him.' This is changed into, 'neither hath it entered into the heart of man *to conceive* the things'. Constantly we hear God addressed as 'the hearer *and answerer* of prayer' – a mere vulgar and useless pleonasm, for the Scripture idea of God's hearing prayer is just his answering it – 'O thou that hearest prayer, unto thee shall all

flesh come'; 'Hear my prayer, O LORD'; 'I love the
LORD because he hath heard my voice and my supplications (*Psa.* 65:2; 39:12; 116:1).

Whence, again, that commonplace of public prayer,
'Thy consolations are neither few nor small.' The reference, I suppose, is to those words of Job, 'Are the
consolations of God small with thee?' (*Job* 15:11). So
one scarce ever hears that prayer of the seventy-fourth
Psalm, 'Have respect to the covenant, for the dark
places of the earth are full of the habitations of cruelty', without the addition, 'horrid cruelty'; nor the
call to prayer in Isaiah, 'Keep not silence, and give
him no rest, till he establish, and till he make Jerusalem a praise in the earth', without the addition, 'the
whole earth'; nor that appeal of the Psalmist, 'Whom
have I in heaven but thee, and there is none upon earth
that I desires beside thee', without the addition, 'none
in all the earth'. So, also, our ear is familiar with 'the
everlasting covenant, well ordered in all things, and
sure'. David's dying words are simply, 'ordered in all
things, and sure.'

These last may, indeed, seem small matters. And so
they are, nor were worth finding fault with, did they
occur but occasionally. But viewed as stereotyped
commonplaces, weak enough in themselves, and
occurring so often as to give an impression of their

having Scripture authority, I humbly think they ought to be discountenanced and discarded, banished wholly from our Presbyterian worship. It will, perhaps, surprise you to learn that the only Scripture authority for that favourite, and somewhat peculiar, expression, about the 'wicked rolling sin as a sweet morsel under their tongue', is the following words in the book of Job (20:12), 'Though wickedness be sweet in his mouth, though he hide it under his tongue.'

Let me venture, in closing, to offer one or two general hints or suggestions, with scarcely any enlargement.

1. There is a certain unity, which, it seems to me, ought to be studied in the entire public service – psalms, prayers, sermon or lecture – all. The very plainness and simplicity which are the glory of our Presbyterian worship urgently demand this, – that pains be taken to impart a certain liveliness, point, *unity*, to the whole service.

2. All-important as the field of intercessory prayer is, let no attempt be made (for it must prove an utter failure), to embrace even any considerable portion of it in any one prayer. Let a certain part be selected, and nothing more supposed to be either necessary or possible.

3. It is a wearisome and useless thing to repeat the whole outline of the sermon in the last prayer. Some reference may and ought to be made to the discourse, but always lightly and briefly.

4. All praying against time, and working of a man's self mechanically up into the spirit of prayer, are to be shunned, as one would shun a viper.

5. Pieces of the English Liturgy seldom suit our mode of prayer. It has a certain measured, stately march of its own, which comports not with the freedom of our prayers.

6. But finally, the *spirit* of prayer must needs lie at the bottom of all, and thus, the cultivating of ceaseless secret prayer, in connection with the blessed Scriptures, whose language forms the very warp and woof of all wise and right public devotion. I speak not of mere texts strung together (which are perhaps the worst kind of public prayers of all), but of a certain vein of Scripture language and thought, running easily, and as it were naturally, through the whole exercise.

I hope you will not imagine that I have come to you about this matter in a self-sufficient spirit. In truth, the things I have thrown out have been the result, very much, of discovered blunders in the course of a long ministry. Confident I am, however, that if the views which have been presented, and the suggestions I have ventured to make, were but acted on over the church at large, the public services would be, to no small extent, revolutionized, and would be characterized by a liveliness, interest, freshness, downright reality and truth, which, as things now are, are often too much lacking.

3

PREACHING: ITS PROPERTIES, PLACE, AND POWER

Let me say two preliminary words before entering on my theme. First, I think most of you have seen an address which I gave some years ago, at a meeting similar to this, on *The connection between godliness and the Christian ministry*. The relation between that theme and the one of this evening is very much that of foundation and superstructure. Oh, remember it well, that godliness is the foundation of all right preaching – as of the entire ministry. It will be wretched preaching, a miserable superstructure, that shall rise on any other foundation than that.

Second, in coming to speak of preaching to you, I hope I may not seem as if saying that I myself have 'attained'. The case is simply this. For forty years I have been a preacher in some sort. I have committed very many blunders: but I have at least been willing to see them. I have striven to rectify and learn from them; and my very blunders have *burned* into me many thoughts about preaching, some of which I would fain give expression to this evening. I can at least promise you this, that you shall have no speculations, no fine-spun theories, from me, but only that which I have made ample proof of, only that which has been with me matter of long and varied experience. I can at least say with Paul, when speaking on another subject, 'Not that I have attained, but I follow after' (*Phil.* 3:12).

1. It is of the *properties* of preaching I desire to speak first, and principally. I pass by those properties which belong to the *matter* of preaching (all-important as they of course are), the great subject-matter of it – Christ crucified, – sin and Christ, – ruin and salvation, – repentance toward God, and faith toward our Lord Jesus Christ, – the whole counsel of God. I limit myself to the *form* (as the old logicians would have said) in contradistinction to the matter. And here, first among the properties of preaching, I mention that it must be –

i. *Direct.* If ever your preaching is to be with power, it must be – in thought, in expression, in utterance – direct, straight for the mark, straight for the hearer; your whole soul, and almost body too, in immediate intercourse with them, eye with eye, face with face, heart with heart. Let it not be a prelection, a speaking in their presence, so much as a speaking *to*, or, better still, *with* them, a solemnly earnest converse, interview, held with them – direct, in short, without any intervening medium.

I think I hear some of you saying, 'Oh, we see what you mean. You wish us to use no manuscript in the pulpit, like yourself.' That, however, is not exactly my meaning. Very possibly some of you may find it best – as I think, unfortunately, yet on the whole the best – to make more or less use of your manuscript in the pulpit. But in this case, I pray you to look well both to the manner in which you prepare the manuscript, and to the manner in which you use it. To the manner of preparing it look well. When you sit down in your study, recollect that your business is to preach, not to compose an essay, or small book. Let your congregation be before your mind's eye from the first. Let that guide your pen, restraining or quickening it as the case may be, throughout.

Beware of a too great facility of writing. There is a dangerous extempore writing, as well as speaking. Remember that your work is not to prepare three quarters of an hour's tolerable instruction, to be submitted to the consideration of your hearers. Your work is to seek their souls, longing after them in the bowels of Jesus Christ. Let this conviction give all possible *directness* alike to your thoughts and to your manner of expressing them. And then, look well to the way in which you use your manuscript in the pulpit. So far as possible, use it as if you did not use it. I speak not, of course, of any miserable attempt to keep it out of view. But what I mean is – see that, by repeated perusals, you get so thorough a hold of it, both in matter and expression, that you shall be pretty much independent of it, shall be no slave to it, shall not require to fix your eye much on it, far less to trace its lines with your finger, but shall be able to keep your eye chiefly on your congregation throughout.

Better far, however – at least, other things being at all equal – if you can dispense with a manuscript altogether. And why not? Reading is not tolerated at the bar, or in the House of Commons, although in both, the object is almost solely to deal with the understanding, to state, and to demonstrate. Doubtless Mr Gladstone made use of no manuscript – anything, I suppose, beyond statistical jottings – even in his three hours' elaborate exposition of last Monday. *Our* work, on the other hand is to reach the inmost heart, to stir the souls of our hearers to their lowest depths, yea, in the case of too many, instrumentally to revolutionize and regenerate them.

For my own part, during these forty years, I have never taken a manuscript to the pulpit. And yet (for I should like here to explain myself a little) I have become very jealous of two things. First, and on the one hand, of extempore speaking, with the aid merely of a prepared skeleton or outline of thoughts; and second, on the other, of committing to memory, and then reciting *memoriter*, a somewhat hastily written manuscript. As to the former method – preaching from a bare outline of thoughts – I am satisfied that, in nine cases out of ten, the preaching will gradually come to be marked by poverty, sameness, pointlessness; and I warn you against it with the utmost earnestness. As for the other method – committing to memory and *memoriter* reciting a manuscript more or less hastily prepared – it is, in the first place, very difficult (although I admit that it may be well in the first instance to grapple with the difficulty, and take this method, for the sake of greater accuracy, as well as for habits of self-denying labour); and, in the second place, the difficulty is too apt to transfer itself to the pulpit, and to be still visible there in that most vacant of all aspects of the human countenance – laborious recollection.

Yet I confess that this latter evil is by no means an unavoidable accompaniment of *memoriter* delivery. Provided the manuscript has been, not hastily, but carefully and leisurely, prepared, wisely prepared also, as respects directness of style, and suitableness otherwise for the pulpit, it may, with due care, be so committed to memory that the preacher, having made it all thoroughly his own, shall be able to give it nearly *verbatim,* without any painful effort, and without the appearance of what I have just called laborious recollection.

My own method has been somewhat of this sort. Of course you must judge for yourselves as to how far to follow it; but principles may be indicated which you may find of use.

When I sit down to prepare for the pulpit, I do not in the first instance make use of pen, ink, and paper. From the first I use a small paper book for pencil jottings of thought and expression. I have my congregation in my eye from the first. When I have hopefully found a text, I try to find a suitable outline or plan – failing of which I throw the whole aside, for the time at least, perhaps transferring the text to a somewhat larger volume kept for texts and thoughts occasionally occurring. If, on the other hand, I find a satisfactory outline, I then try to gather materials, ample materials, under the different parts of it. I do not for the present write – save as to those pencil jottings, more or fewer, of thought and expression – but *I preach mentally to my congregation.* I *do* write, in a sense, but the paper, or writing-table, is the mind. Substantially the composition is a series of mental preachings, at the first rude, rough, and unpromising, but gradually taking shape, order, and proportion.

Then on the Saturday I could without much difficulty transfer the whole in writing to one of a series of larger volumes in which I preserve my discourses. Usually, however, I prefer reserving this for the Monday, after preaching. But what I wish you particularly to note is, that now in the pulpit, and after this kind of preparation, I find, first, that in place of any lack of *expression,* I have rather to make a choice between different modes of it that have occurred to me; and second, that it is no longer a mere exercise of memory, but of memory, judgment, emotion, association of ideas - all the faculties of the mind together. It is now just an easier and more effective thinking, arguing, expostulating, appealing, beseeching, by the aid of the whole previous meditation of thoughts and expressions. This I am well persuaded of, that the best of all modes of preaching would be an easy, fully premeditated, solemn, earnest, direct, converse with the hearers. I would have said *conversation,* but that there is an artificial association of that word with a certain free and easy chit-chat.

The association, however, is altogether artificial; for why should conversation not be grave and solemn in the highest degree? Everything depends on the subject. If I come to converse with you about matters involving my good name, or property, or life, depend on it, there will be no chit-chat. There will be no declamation, indeed, no mere oratory, *as such,* and for its own sake. But there will be all possible room for pathos, power, *eloquence*, in the only true sense of the word.

But whatever method you may take in detail, let your preaching be, as I said in entering on this particular, *direct,* in thought, in expression, in utterance, your whole soul and very eyes in immediate intercourse with your hearers. John Livingstone somewhere writes, 'I was more helped in my preaching by the thirsty eyes of the people than by anything else.'

ii. Second, *scriptureful.* I am obliged to coin a word here, because I do not mean scriptural, but largely clothed in Scripture language, scriptural thoughts conveyed, to a large extent, in the very words of the sacred volume. Only I would not be misunderstood, as if it were meant that discourses are to be *anyhow* full of Scripture. It is true that no discourse will be according to what I humbly judge to be the right model of preaching which has not much Scripture in it. But the *converse* by no means holds, that any discourse which has a great deal of Scripture in it must be a good one. Nay, there is scarcely any kind of preaching more poor and pointless than that in which portions of Scripture are strung together, and made to do duty in the way of supplying the preacher's poverty of thought. If Scripture texts are, as I believe them to be, the gems of preaching, yet they must be in right setting, else they shall not give forth their brightness and beauty.

These 'apples of gold', to change the figure, must be 'in a frame-work of silver'. If the words of Scripture are the arrows, as I believe they are, which chiefly reach the heart, yet they shall fall to the ground ineffectual, unless they are skilfully *feathered* and discharged from the bow. Scripture texts are eminently the baits of our 'fishing'; yet in the hands of a slovenly and unskilful fisherman they will miserably fail of attracting and 'catching men'. And yet they *are* the gems, the arrows, the baits. Oh, if you would preach well, acquaint yourselves, I beseech you, with this blessed volume. Literally get it *by heart*; delight much in it; learn to say of it, 'I rejoice at thy word, as one that findeth great spoil' (*Psa.* 119:162) – 'Thy words were found, and I did eat them; and thy word was unto me the joy and rejoicing of mine heart' (*Jer.* 15:16). Strive to be able to quote Scripture with ease, and with accuracy. And (more expressly to my present purpose), when you sit down to prepare for the pulpit, make large use of such a book as Bagster's *Treasury of Scripture References and Parallel Passages.*

I spoke of gathering materials under the different parts of your outline. Let them consist largely of the best parallels under each. You shall find the time thoroughly well spent in such gathering. Whether it be for explanatory statement, or for proof, or for illustration, or for application to the conscience and heart, the words of Scripture will be found to supply the choicest of all materials. Of them I would say what David said of Goliath's sword, 'There is none like that, give it me.'

No doubt men of genius, being godly men also, may preach admirable discourses without much Scripture in them. Although I do not apprehend that they are formed after the right model of preaching, still they may be noble discourses; and commonplace men may soon make fools of themselves by trying to copy after the style of them. But then, what is to come of the average ministry of a church unless Scripture be made large and skilful use of? For my own part, so highly do I esteem the language of the Scriptures as an instrument of preaching, that were I to live fifty years longer, I believe I could make continual advance in the work of preaching, simply from having learned to draw much on the exhaustless treasury of the Word of God.

iii. Third, e*asy to be understood.* I might have first said, easy to be *heard,* an important matter truly, and deserving the most careful study, a clear and distinct articulation.[1] But I content myself with saying *easy to be understood.* Possibly, indeed, the preacher has no thoughts much worth understanding. In this case I can only say to him, seek after better ones; and, if you have not mistaken your calling, and shall ask better thoughts from God, and take due pains, you shall find them. But supposing that you have thoughts not unworthy of being listened to, then strive to clothe them in good, plain English.

I place *easy to be understood* in opposition to three different things. First, to a certain slovenly, slipshod, hazy, obscure style of expression, where the hearer

---

[1] See Dean Ramsay's interesting and valuable letter on *The Art of Reading and Preaching Distinctly.* R. Grant & Co., Edinburgh.

cannot, for the life of him, see what you would be at, and feels as if you had led him into a wood, from which if he is to make his escape he had better part company with you. But, secondly, I place *easy to be understood*, in opposition to fine, learned, scientific, high-sounding, sesquipedalian[1] words, which really are good for nothing but to conceal poverty of thought. And be assured that the *omne ignotum pro magnifico*[2] is of very short duration. People soon come to see through it. Oh for the Anglo-Saxon of Bunyan's *Pilgrim*, or of Spurgeon's *John Ploughman's Talk* – a book, by the way, of the highest value, alike for its thoughts and its singularly graphic and lucid style, fitting it equally for a palace and a hovel.

Still further, I place *easy to be understood* in opposition to a certain naked, bare, too logically accurate, manner of expression, which fails to lodge the thoughts in the mind of the hearer, and as it were fasten the nail.

It will often be found of high importance to seek out several adjectives, not quite synonymous, yet homogeneous, which, by their rapid succession, shall carry the thought fully home to the apprehension of

[1] Sesquipedalian: long and pedantic.

[2] *omne ignotum pro magnifico*: everything unknown is taken for magnificent, i.e., being impressed with the mere sound of words.

the hearer. I have long been accustomed to make a good deal of use, in this matter, of Roget's *Thesaurus of English Words and Phrases,* and would commend it much to your notice. But now, and in close connection with *easy to be understood,* let me mark another property of preaching.

iv. Fourth, *lively.* In thought, in expression, and in utterance, let your preaching be life-like, warm, spirited. I do not say loud, remember, but lively. Still less do I mean smart, jaunty, but lively, in opposition to flat, tame, heavy, pointless, prosing, tedious, wearisome. I mean what the ancients called *vis vivida.*[1] The French excel us greatly in this. It might seem, indeed, that our Scottish *perfervidum ingenium*[2] should secure this property of preaching. But then, we are so metaphysical and argumentative! In the first part of my own ministry I used never to think a sermon worth much unless it were charged everywhere with formal argument. Long ago, however, I have learned to satisfy myself with the *substance* of argument, and to throw its mere forms and dress away. The Scottish *perfervidum ingenium* combined with the vivacity of the French would make an

[1] *Vis vivida:* lively force or vigour.
[2] *Perfervidum ingenium:* intensely earnest character.

invaluable compound. And be assured that this is a matter of the last importance, belonging, as it vitally does, to the fixing and sustaining of the people's attention. We have this last, I am persuaded, very much in our own power.

No doubt there is a higher attention we cannot command, that of which it is written, 'the Lord opened the heart of Lydia, that she attended to the things spoken by Paul' (*Acts* 16:14). But I believe that we have it largely in our power to arrest and sustain the mere attention of our hearers. For this end we must learn to feel their pulse, as it were, to mark when their attention begins to flag, and by various means recall and keep it. The first property of preaching which I mentioned is most vital here – directness, direct intercourse between the preacher and the hearers. Why, think of the etymology of our word *interesting*, that in which the hearer is made to feel he has an interest, a share, a part. In the book of Ecclesiastes there is a text of the highest value here, 'The words of the wise are as goads, and as nails fastened by the masters of assemblies, which are given from one shepherd.'

v. Fifth, *assured, indubious*. I am unwilling to say dogmatic, and loath even to say authoritative; but I say *assured* or *indubious,* and yet modest and humble. Certainly I do not mean self-asserting, self-sufficient, pretentious. But I place *assured* in opposition to a certain timid and hesitating tone – 'for if the trumpet give an uncertain sound, who shall prepare himself for the battle?' (*1 Cor.* 14:8). No doubt, if you are to preach your own opinions and speculations to the people, submit them, by all means, very humbly for their consideration. But, I beseech you, learn to preach in the spirit of those words, 'We cannot but speak the things which we have seen and heard' – 'That which we have seen and heard declare we unto you' – 'We know that the Son of God is come, and hath given us an understanding, that we may know him that is true' – 'We believe and are sure that thou art that Christ, the Son of the living God' (*Acts* 4:20; *1 John* 1:3; 5:20; *John* 6:69).

Long I have valued a passage in the book of Acts as full of instruction here. It is said of Paul that he 'went into the synagogue of the Jews, and three Sabbath days reasoned with them *out of the Scriptures, opening and alleging* that Christ must needs have suffered', etc. (*Acts* 17:2–3) – first 'opening', *then* 'alleging'. Ah! when you have first of all 'opened', out of the Scriptures, then you may 'allege' as confidently as you please. As a kind of balancing force, however, I added *modest and humble*. The whole you have in Paul's great and well-known words, 'All things are of God, who hath reconciled us to himself by Jesus Christ, and hath given to us the ministry of reconciliation; to wit, that God was in Christ reconciling the world unto himself, not imputing their trespasses unto them; and hath committed unto us the word of reconciliation. Now then we are ambassadors for Christ, as though God did beseech you by us: we pray you in Christ's stead, be ye reconciled to God. For he hath made him to be sin for us, who knew no sin; that we might be made the righteousness of God in him' (2 *Cor.* 5:18–21).

vi. Sixth, *aiming ever at the grand objects and ends*. Fain I would have found a single word to express this. But had I said practical, it might have seemed as if in contradistinction to *doctrinal*, whereas there may be that which is thoroughly speculative about practice, or duty, just as much as what is thoroughly practical about doctrine – of which last let me give one example to bring out what I have in view: 'I am the resurrection and the life; he that believeth in me, though he were dead, yet shall he live; and whosoever liveth and believeth in me shall never die. *Believest thou this*?' (*John* 11:25–26).

Oh, see to it that, whether you are dealing with doctrine or duty, faith or life, your preaching be throughout pervaded by personal application – How is it with you, dear hearer? Lord, is it I? Search me, O God, and know my heart, try me, and know my thoughts! Few things are in the whole ministry either harder, or more momentous, than bearing continually in mind the grand end, the conversion and salvation of souls, and aiming deliberately at it, while we preach, in contradistinction to any mere comfortable discharge of so much duty and work. And thus I notice one other property.

vii. Seventh, *bathed in prayer*. I mark this as a property of preaching, because I do not simply mean that you yourselves be men of prayer, but that your discourses, your whole preaching, be steeped and bathed in prayer. Oh, seek your texts in prayer. Carry your whole preparations on in prayer. Strive to preach in the spirit of prayer.

You might find it of great use here to gather together some *materials of request* in reference to pulpit preparation and pulpit work. As I have nothing but your good in view, I am not afraid of being misunderstood if I mention that long I have been accustomed to keep by me a considerable number of gathered materials of request, for frequent reference and use in connection with preparations for the pulpit. Please take the following as examples of them:

Come with me, and I will make you to become fishers of men – Fear not, from henceforth thou shalt catch men.

Tenderness and faithfulness – Solemnity not loudness – Humility and modesty – *Pectus est quod theologum facit*[1] – Reality – Self forgotten and crucified.

Feed my sheep, feed my *lambs*.

Forsake not the messenger nor the message - carry him through, and it home.

Be not afraid of their faces, *for* I am with thee – be not dismayed at their faces, *lest* I confound thee before them.

Not wisdom of words, but *words* of wisdom – wise to win souls.

On no account satisfied with preparations, or preaching, or acceptance, apart from the end – souls, to the glory of God.

---

[1] *Pectus est quod theologum facit:* It is the heart that makes the theologian.

Use and usefulness of preparations, both from God.

In brief addition to what I have said on the properties of preaching, let me rapidly offer a few separate hints on *preparation for the pulpit*.

First, *find time for it*. Whatever may be your other occupations, you must take, and find, sufficient time to prepare for the pulpit. The longer I preach I am the more convinced that this is a simple necessity in order to all good preaching.

Second, *distinguish carefully between the Lecture and the Sermon*. Unhappily the whole idea of the Lecture seems in danger of going out among us. It becomes very much a kind of sermon, or rather two or three little sermons, on a simply longer text. Recollect, however, that the proper and distinctive idea of the Sermon is exposition – not, indeed, a mere running comment, such as might usefully be given in a drawing-room, or at a prayer-meeting, but still an exposition, with full illustration and application throughout.

Third, in the sermon, more especially, let there be a certain *unity*, so that the discourse might have a title given to it. Of course there ought to be diversity in the unity; yet a certain unity is essential to a good sermon.

Fourth, let the sermon be ordinarily *textual*, in the sense of both the unity and the diversity being drawn out of the text, and in such a manner corresponding with and relating to it that the discourse could not well be preached from any other text than its own. For myself, I have scarce half-a-dozen sermons in my possession which could be preached from other texts than those from which they were written.

Fifth, labour to find *a good plan or outline, and let the plan be your own.* You shall make very little of such skeletons as those in Simeon's volumes, for example. The plan must be your own, and it must take a firm hold of your mind, else you shall not make much of it [see Appendix, 1].

Finally, remember what I before said as to *gathering ample materials, under each part of the plan.* And my own idea very strongly is that it is best to have a pretty full mental conception of the entire discourse before doing much in the way of writing. The best painters, I believe, proceed thus with their works, conceiving their pictures first as a whole mentally. So also is it with the highest musical compositions. I happened lately to meet with an interesting fact respecting Mendelssohn: He 'always composed in his head, and never at the piano. Like Mozart, every piece of music, with all its instrumentation, was in his mind before he wrote it down. Sometimes an idea occurred to him when seated at the piano, which he then hastily noted down, and subsequently resumed and worked out in his head' (Elise Polko, *Reminiscences of Mendelssohn*, translated by Lady Wallace).

And now I have to touch (though too briefly) on the *place*, and on the *power*, of preaching.

2. Its *place*. Assuredly, in the work of the Christian ministry, the place which preaching holds is an altogether central one. It is not wonderful, of course, if an opposite opinion be held by those who think that they can regenerate their fellows by simply baptizing them. But let us who regard everything of this kind as a dream, rest in Paul's words, 'Christ sent me not to baptize, but to preach the gospel' (*1 Cor.* 1:17). Then, if preaching be compared with pastoral visitation, I will only say this respecting it, that the domestic visitation of the flock is doubtless a work of vast importance – one on which I could willingly say much, if this were the occasion for it [see Appendix, 2]. And yet the most diligent household visitation throughout the week will be of little power without good preaching on the Sabbath. Pastoral work among the families of the flock is the complement – *but it is nothing more* – the exceedingly precious supplement

and complement, of the effective preaching of the Word on Sabbath. As to public *prayer*, I do not enter into any comparison of preaching with it, because I am dealing simply with the minister's own work, whereas the public prayers are, or ought to be, the work of the congregation, in a sort, quite as much as of the minister. As such, however, it were very difficult to overestimate its importance. The address on Public Prayer, which, seven years ago, I delivered at a meeting of your College Missionary Association, and which was afterwards published at the request of the Elders' Conference, I venture earnestly and affectionately to commend to your attention [see chapter 2].

3. The *power of preaching*. But we are told that this in our age is gone, the Press having taken its place. If so, assuredly the worse for the age; for the Press, whatever may be its power, can never supply the place of the Pulpit. But I believe that this whole allegation about the power of the Pulpit being gone is baseless. I will tell you what is gone. The power of a neat little manuscript, carried to the pulpit, and prettily read – that is gone. Oh, never attempt, by the reading of a little manuscript book in the pulpit, to compete with the volumes which issue from the

press, or you shall be miserably cast in the competition.

But carry to the pulpit *a different thing altogether*; carry to it well-digested thoughts, with suitable words to express them – written in your inmost soul, and if needful also in your manuscript – thoughts and words wherewith to stir the souls of your hearers to their inmost depths, – wherewith to hold living intercourse with them, and tell them what God has been telling *you*; and both you and they shall find that the Pulpit still wields a power altogether its own.

As for the Press, I am confident that in this age of rapid communication, and ceaseless living intercourse of man with man, books are not *actually read* to any such extent as is apt to be imagined. A few are read carefully through. A much larger number are glanced over. And larger and older works are used for reference. But it is the weekly or monthly magazine, with the 'article' written yesterday for to-day's newspaper, that is chiefly read.

Is not this to be regretted? Possibly it may; but so the fact is. And thus I am persuaded that, so far from the power of the Pulpit being gone, things are ripe at this hour for its exercising a greater power than perhaps ever before, if we ministers be but true to ourselves, and our blessed office and work.

I have done. You may have heard of the English traveller, who, when sitting beside the driver, in the old days of the mail-coach, and having asked him various questions about the places on the road, was again and again answered, 'I don't know, Sir.' Fretted at length with the ignorance of the man, he said, 'Do you know anything?' 'Yes, Sir,' he replied, '*how to drive the coach*.' Oh, you may have all the learning in the world in your heads, but it shall avail you nothing for the work of the ministry, if you have not learned to *preach*.

Two things are indispensable to make a minister – first, that he be a Christian; second, that he be a Preacher.

May you be greatly blessed to roll back that reproach of the Pulpit in our day, that its power is gone! Far, far otherwise is the fact; and do you help to prove it. The Lord give you understanding in all things!

4

ELEMENTS OF PULPIT POWER[1]

I have felt a kind of 'necessity laid upon me' not to lose the opportunity I enjoy this evening once for all, of giving utterance to what, amid all the imperfections of my own ministry, has been little short of a ruling passion with me these many years past – even to see a higher and higher standard among us of ministerial, and specifically of pulpit, power. It may be permitted to me from this place to say a few things to my younger brethren in the ministry, and to our probationers and students, in answer to this question – Wherein chiefly lie the elements of power, and correspondingly of weakness, in the pulpit? I reply to the question:

1. First, assuredly, in the *personal character* of the man who fills the pulpit. This cannot need to be *proved* – it is much too obvious. But it very greatly needs to be believed, to be felt and realized. It will be

[1] Extract from closing address to the Free Church of Scotland General Assembly.

acknowledged at once that that minister whose life is not in fair harmony with his pulpit teaching, had as well, for any good he is likely to do, cease to be a teacher. And here I do not point merely to that solemn first principle respecting the ministry, that conversion to God lies necessarily at the bottom of it – that he who will be a servant of Christ officially must be his servant first personally – that he who would be an ambassador to negotiate peace between God and his rebel subjects must himself have ceased to be of their number. But, over and above, I point to the spirit of all such words, in him who fills the pulpit, as those – 'Tell me, O thou whom my soul loveth, where thou feedest, where thou makest thy flock to rest at noon.' 'My soul thirsteth for God, for the living God.' 'Set me as a seal upon thine heart, as a seal upon thine arm; for love is strong as death, jealousy is cruel as the grave.' 'Oh, that my ways were directed to keep thy statutes!' (*Song of Sol.* 1:7; *Psa.* 42:2; *Song of Sol.* 8:6; *Psa.* 119:5).

Alas for the power of that minister's pulpit about whom even suspicions can get abroad of his worldly-mindedness, or his levity of deportment, or his want of scrupulous veracity, or temperance, or his indifference to the welfare of his people! But then I do not speak of the absence simply of everything of that kind, but of the positive manifest presence of at least earnest longings after that spirit, 'To me to live is Christ'; 'This one thing I do, forgetting those things which are behind, and reaching forth to those things which are before, I press toward the mark for the prize of the high calling of God in Christ Jesus' (*Phil.* 1:21; 3:14). Will you allow me to read here a short passage from Bunyan's *Pilgrim*, very humbling, indeed, and fitted, I fear, to draw from too many of us the cry, 'My leanness, my leanness!' yet very precious:

Then said the Interpreter, 'Come in; I will show thee that which will be profitable to thee.' So he commanded his man to light the candle, and bid Christian follow him. So he had him into a private room, and bid his man open a door; the which when he had done, Christian saw a picture of a very grave person hang up against the wall, and this was the fashion of it. – It had eyes lifted up to heaven; the best of books in its hand; the law of truth was written upon its lips; the world was behind his back; it stood as if it pleaded with men, and a crown of gold did hang over its head.

Then said Christian, 'What means this?'

Interpreter. The man whose picture this is, is one of a thousand. He can beget children, travail in birth with children, and nurse them himself when they are born. And whereas thou seest him with eyes 'lifted up to Heaven, the best of books in his hand, and the law of truth writ on his lips', it is to show thee that his work is to know and unfold dark things to sinners, even as also thou seest him 'stand as if he pleaded with men'; and whereas thou seest the world as cast behind him, and that a crown hangs over his head, that is to show thee that, slighting and despising the things that are present, for the love that he hath to his master's service, he is sure in the world that comes next, to have glory for his reward. Now, said the Interpreter, I have showed thee this picture first, because the man whose picture this is, is the only man whom the lord of the place whither thou art going hath authorized to be thy guide in all difficult places thou mayest meet with in the way; wherefore take good heed to what I have showed thee, and bear well in thy mind what thou hast seen, lest in thy journey thou meet with some that pretend to lead thee right, but their way goes down to death.

'Search me, O God, and know my heart; try me, and know my thoughts'! 'Deliver me from blood-guiltiness, O God, thou God of my salvation, and my tongue shall sing aloud of thy righteousness'! (*Psa.* 139:23; 51:14).

2. But, second, to the question wherein chiefly lie the elements of power, and correspondingly of weakness, in the pulpit, I answer in *the kind of prayers* which are offered in it.

Perhaps some one is ready to say, O then, if the power of the pulpit depends so much on the kind of prayers offered in it, why not secure their being always of the right kind by adopting a liturgy? Now I cannot certainly content myself with replying, that, in point of fact, such is not our method in Scotland. I rejoice greatly that it is not our method. The use of a prescribed form for even part of our public service I should wholly deprecate. And had I my ministry to begin again, in place of having it soon to close, it would be a simple joy to me to think of possibly twenty or thirty years more of Sabbath ministration with our method of free and unread prayers. But then just the more that they are free and unread, I the more earnestly plead for this whole department of our public service receiving a great deal more attention and care than have, I fear, been usually bestowed on it.

Why, just think of a minister's going to his pulpit to lead his entire congregation, in a sense, by his prayers to the divine throne, the blood-sprinkled mercy-seat! Never will things be among us as they ought, until it shall be held simply unlawful before God to enter the pulpit (save in exceptional cases) without serious forethought as to the prayers which are to be offered in it. I speak of no composing of prayers – writing out of prayers to be committed to memory. Oh no. But I do speak of the premeditation, more or less, of some general line, at least, of devotional thought and utterance, whereby, first, the minister shall be no more as if at sea without compass or rudder, to wander over all sorts of things; and whereby, second, in place of being anywise cramped and confined, he shall be left just the more free to listen to the faintest breathings of the good Spirit of God, 'the Spirit of grace and supplications' (*Zech.* 12:10).

I must be allowed from this place to declare myself (as I have done elsewhere) the enemy of *long prayers in public*. Oh, we shall not easily pray too long in secret. We shall not easily pray too long when we have entered into our closet and shut our door behind us. But, according to my humble judgment, we shall probably pray too long if we ordinarily pray in public – of course I mean in a single devotional exercise – more than eight or ten minutes. No doubt a good man might be longer in the spirit of public prayer himself. But he shall not easily carry his people longer with him in that spirit. I also venture humbly, but very firmly, to protest against all such prayers as are rather a kind of preachings, or at best devout meditatings, in place of being, more or less, what the public prayers of Robert Bruce of Edinburgh are described as having been, like 'bolts shot up to heaven'. And are we never to see an end of the 'Presbyterian liturgy' – as it has been quietly called – those very poor traditionary, conventional phrases, handed down somehow from generation to generation, and made up of mangled Scripture texts, torn from their connection, and pieced together to do duty in the service of the sanctuary.

Weakness in the pulpit! No wonder the whole service is weakened nearly to death if the people are to be wearied out by the prayers before the sermon has even begun. I may be allowed respectfully to commend to attention my own 'Address on Public Prayer', which unhappily has not become superfluous since 1862, when it was delivered to the students of the Edinburgh New College [see chapter 2]..

3. Third, to the question wherein chiefly lie the elements of power, and correspondingly of weakness, in the pulpit, I answer, in the minister's aiming consciously and deliberately *at the right ends,* both in

his preparations for the pulpit and in his preaching from it. Aiming at the right ends. Neither can this possibly require to be proved, but only to be believed, realized, practised.

For we are fishermen. 'Come after me', said Jesus, 'and I will make you fishers of men' (*Matt.* 4:19; *Mark* 1:17). But what fisherman ever thought of taking his lines, and preparing his hooks and baits, and going down to the water, and laboriously fishing, indifferent all the while about any result – about the taking of fish? And here I do not point, on the opposite side, to any such low and simply despicable ends as 'entering the priest's office', and preaching, 'for a bit of bread'. Oh, the ministry, as one said, the most honourable of professions, is the most dishonourable of trades. But then, unhappily, there are intermediate ends betwixt that and the true one of the saving of precious souls, very subtle and plausible for our poor hearts, and in which we are but too apt to settle down content.

Especially there is the end of what is called 'doing our duty', 'getting comfortably and acceptably through our work'. Ah, doing our duty, getting comfortably through our work! But what of the souls, meanwhile, that are either saved or lost? I remember Luther says somewhere in his *Table-talk*, 'Though I am now an old man, and accustomed to preaching, I tremble as often as I enter the pulpit.' Does any say, Duty is ours, issues are God's – the saving of souls lies not with us, but with the sovereign God? But I say that God's holy sovereignty is simply abused and prostituted when it is made a cover for our sin in not aiming consciously and deliberately at the end of our whole work together, 'I will make you fishers *of men*' – 'I send thee to open their eyes, to turn them from darkness to light, and from the power of Satan unto God, that they may receive forgiveness of sins, and inheritance among them that are sanctified, by faith that is in me' (*Matt.* 4:19; *Acts* 26:18).

And I said, aiming at the right ends in our preparations for the pulpit, as well as our preaching from it. In truth, the ends aimed at will determine largely the whole kind and character of the preparations. If the end be anything short of saving our people's souls, then plenty of room will be found for neat sentences, and well-rounded periods of mere words, and other things which, with that end steadily in view, would simply appear altogether out of place, while, *for* that end, other and far different things would irresistibly suggest themselves to be thrown in from time to time, such as, Are you saved, my dear hearer? – Are you born again? – How is it with you and with me? etc.

4. But fourth, and very intimately connected with aiming at the right ends, to the question, wherein chiefly lie the elements of power, and correspondingly of weakness, in the pulpit, I answer, in the minister's *apprehending the strength by which, and the kind of words by means of which*, the ends are to be obtained. Apprehending the strength *by* which: No fears of this, if the ends themselves are but realized and aimed at. 'Son of man, can these bones live? And I answered, O Lord God, thou knowest' (*Ezek.* 37:3) – certainly, Lord, by no power less than thine – 'God, which quickeneth the dead, and calleth the things which be not, as though they were' – 'That ye may know what is the exceeding greatness of his power to usward who believe, according to the working of his mighty power, which he wrought in Christ when he raised him from the dead . . . and [raised] you who were dead in trespasses and sins' (*Rom.* 4:17; *Eph.* 1:18–20, 2:1).

But then, if God's omnipotency alone can accomplish the ends, may we not be at least somewhat less anxious about the *kind of words* by means of which they may be attained? Nay, not at all the less; for it is written – and I care nothing about the *quomodo* [how] here, enough to know the *quod* [what] – that Paul and Barnabas went into the synagogue of

Iconium, 'and so spake that' (λαλησαι ουτως ωστε πιστευσαι – in such a manner spake as that) 'a great multitude, both of the Jews and also of the Greeks, believed' (*Acts* 14:1).

Three things here, in the very briefest manner, about the kind of words. That they be, first, words expressive of living thoughts – arousing, searching, directing, comforting, as the case may be – gathered out of the storehouse of this blessed volume. In fact, in the first instance when preparations are entered on, the mere words may be left to shift very much for themselves. Thoughts chiefly are to be sought, materials of ample thought, together with a simple and natural outline, or plan, according to which to arrange them. But *now,* second, words have become of nearly as much moment as thoughts, because the hearer can know your thoughts only by your words. Style, which is just nothing for its own sake, is a very great deal as the vehicle of thought, for the lodging of it in the hearer's soul. Have you got thoughts? Then with all care seek words, clear, telling, burning, appropriate, and to be uttered audibly, pleasingly, articulately, by which to convey them. And, third, let both thoughts and words go straight from you to your congregation, without any intervening *media* to carry off the force – without, I take leave to say –

without, if it be at all possible, a read manuscript intervening, to draw your eyes down, and off from the eyes of your hearers. 'I was more helped in my preaching', said John Livingstone once, 'by the thirsty eyes of the people than by anything else.'

On this somewhat delicate subject I will only say this. I venture to predict that after I am dead and gone, if the power of the pulpit in Scotland is to continue and to grow, read sermons, save in exceptional cases, will be discarded, even as reading from a manuscript is quite unknown both in the senate and at the bar. I think I have taken as much pains as most men with my pulpit preparations these forty-one years. Oh, they have been, and are at this day as much as ever, a very enthusiasm, passion, with me – scarce one Sabbath's work over when I am into that of another. But I never read a sermon in my life; and the recollection assuredly has no place among the things I look back on with regret.

5. Fifth, and very briefly, to the question, wherein chiefly lie the elements of power, and correspondingly of weakness, in the pulpit, I answer, in the offering of *much prayer about the weekly preparations* for it, and specifically, at the close of them on a Saturday evening. Oh, blessed Saturday evenings,

in which the minister, after his preparations have been pretty well completed, shall turn to such a chapter as Matthew 14, and shall pray over those words (taken in their abiding principles), 'He said unto them, They need not depart; give ye them to eat. And they say unto him, We have here but five loaves and two fishes. He said, BRING THEM HITHER TO ME. And he commanded the multitude to sit down on the grass; and took the five loaves and the two fishes, and, looking up to heaven, he blessed, and break; and gave the loaves to his disciples, and the disciples to the multitude' (*Matt.* 14:16–19).

Or that blessed passage in Exodus 33: 'Moses said unto the LORD, See, thou sayest unto me, Bring up this people: and thou hast not let me know whom thou wilt send with me. Yet thou hast said, I know thee by name, and thou hast also found grace in my sight. Now therefore, I pray thee, if I have found grace in thy sight, show me now thy way, that I may know thee, that I may find grace in thy sight; and consider that this nation is thy people. And he said, My presence shall go with thee, and I will give thee rest. And he said unto him, If thy presence go not with me, carry us not up hence' (*Exod.* 33:12–15).

Or that word in 1 Thessalonians, first chapter, 'Our gospel came not unto you in word only, but also in power, and in the Holy Ghost, and in much assurance' (*1 Thess.* 1:5). Or – one other example – that great word in the beginning of Acts, He 'commanded them that they should not depart from Jerusalem, but *wait for the promise of the Father,* which, saith he, ye have heard of me: for John truly baptized with water; but ye shall be baptized with the Holy Ghost, not many days hence' (*Acts* 1:4–5). The offering of much prayer, I say, about our weekly preparations, and specifically, at the close of them on a Saturday evening.

6. Sixth, and last, to the question, wherein lie the elements of power, and correspondingly of weakness, in the pulpit, I answer *in the minister's command (or want of command) of the sword of the Spirit, which is the Word of God* – command of this grand weapon, instrument, of our whole ministry, the holy Scriptures. Manifestly such command of our sword, our weapon, must lie greatly in our own faith in it – unquestioning confidence in the Bible, as not the word of man, but in very truth the Word of God, which effectually worketh also in them that believe (*1 Thess.* 2:13).

And this confidence is not to be attained by the reading of ever so many books on the evidences, half so much as by a blessed, ever-growing, experimental acquaintance with the Scriptures, in their exceeding glory, and divine suitableness to all the necessities of our own case. Ah, there it is – 'I rejoice at thy word, as one that findeth great spoil.' 'How, sweet are thy words unto my taste! yea, sweeter than honey to my mouth!' 'Thy words were found, and I did eat them; and thy word was unto me the joy and rejoicing of mine heart' (*Psa.* 119:162; 119:103; *Jer.* 15:16).

And thus shall we acquire a greater and greater command of our weapon in this other way, that a large and ever increasing portion of the Scriptures shall come to be literally *gotten by heart* – fixed, I mean, in our memory by means of our heart, – by means of an acquaintance with it so intimate and loving that we shall be more than able to quote it accurately – scarcely able, in fact to quote it otherwise. And the importance of this last who shall tell, if the fact be, as I am profoundly convinced it is, that the best of all materials of preaching, whether for explanation, or proof, or illustration, or application, are the very words of Scripture, selected with spiritual skill; carefully managed as to *the setting*, so to speak (for they are gems – the 'feathering of the arrows', as one called it, using a different figure); and uttered forth from the preacher's inmost heart?

But enough. I might have spoken of many other things, such as the vast importance *of reading Scripture well* – reading it clearly, intelligently, naturally, solemnly, impressively. But I forbear. I have spoken only of the pulpit.

I may be allowed to commend to my younger brethren, and to our probationers and students, some thoughts on Communion-table addresses, and on pastoral visitation, which will be found in the appendix which immediately follows.

APPENDIX:

1. PLAN OF SERMONS – INTRODUCTION – CONCLUSION

Having been obliged, in the address on Preaching, to touch too briefly on the plan or outline of sermons, I should like to enlarge a little on it here, adding a sentence or two on Introduction and Conclusion.

1. As to plan or outline, I am persuaded, generally, that too much pains can scarce be bestowed on it. Whether the preacher is to announce his plan formally or no, let him strive at least to *have* a plan, and one of the most definite character, in his mind. And, although both the propriety and the manner of announcing it must depend very much on circumstances, such as the character of it, the subject of the discourse, and the measure of intelligence in the audience, yet I am satisfied that it is best, as a general rule, distinctly to announce the plan near the opening.

Then, more specifically, first, let there be *no mechanical observing of any fixed and unvarying method* in the preacher's outlines. An endless variety will naturally arise here from the character of the text and of the theme, which ought ever to guide, as to his specific plan.

Secondly, the method ought thus to be always *natural* – not usually, indeed, such as would have occurred to anybody, but yet simple when announced, and easily and thoroughly intelligible. It is most desirable, no doubt, to avoid the commonplace in outlines; and if such a measure of care is taken, and thought bestowed, as the importance of the matter deserves, this ordinarily should not be found very difficult. Never, however, let the desire of shunning the commonplace land the preacher in plans subtle, artificial, abstruse. The whole end of them were thus defeated, and the benefit lost.

In like manner, thirdly, let the plan be *light* and *easy* – not cumbrous, lumbering, heavy. If it is wished to put the audience early to sleep, the preacher has but to announce a sufficiently large and ponderous method or plan. Let care be taken not to multiply *heads* of discourse. If there are three, it will be best usually not to subdivide them – certainly not the whole of them. If there are but two, subdivision will be more than admissible, often it will be very desirable.

But without heads, an excellent plan is sometimes obtained by means of a series of successive particulars – five, six, or even seven, if the illustrations are not much prolonged. And, finally, let the entire plan be *congruous with the spirit of the text and of the theme*. It is not easy to express in words what is meant by this. But the painstaking preacher will come to understand it, and the high importance of it.

It belongs very much to that unity which, along with a due diversity, forms so prominent a characteristic of every good sermon.

2. *Introduction* and *Conclusion*. As to the former, how evident it seems, and yet how often and lamentably forgotten, that the only use of an introduction is just suitably to *introduce*, or make way for, the discourse which is to follow. The young preacher, justly attaching great importance to a good opening, is tempted to labour at his introduction, and prolong it, to the serious injury of his whole sermon. Far better no introduction than this. And occasionally it is really best to dispense with introduction, to dash at once into the theme, and announce the plan. Much oftener, however, some introduction is desirable, and its constant absence would betoken indolence and bad taste.

Only let it be simple and brief – its character and matter being suggested naturally by the text, the theme, or the proposed method – so that both preacher and hearers may pass without weariness, to the body of the discourse, and be led to keep each other pleasant company throughout. Many years ago

I recollect my friend Dr Guthrie telling me, when we were on a tour in Ireland, how, when beginning his ministry in the country parish of Arbirlot, he observed the tendency of the labouring people to get drowsy near the opening of the sermon, and so learned always to begin with something striking, if not startling – some arresting incident, or similitude, or illustration.

I venture, however, to recommend to ordinary preachers a most cautious and sparing use of this manner of arresting attention in the opening sentence, lest there follow a painful reaction and collapse. For my admirable friend, with his endless command of illustration, the plan was excellent. But I am persuaded that, as a general rule, a brief introduction, carefully weighed, easy, somewhat quiet in character – and withal natural, simply from its having struck the preacher as a suitable way of getting into the body of his discourse – will be found the best.

As to *Conclusion* – assuredly if a right beginning of anything is of much moment, no less important a right and suitable ending of it. And first here, our old writers are certainly not to be followed by use in those long and detailed 'application' and 'uses' with which they in effect preached their sermons over again before they reached the close. This were not only unsuitable to the tastes and habits of our day, but I can see no special advantage that should arise from it, judging the question simply on its merits. On the other hand, however, I have no doubt that the abrupt manner in which some esteemed modern preachers are accustomed to close their discourses the instant they have finished the filling up of their outline, is a mistake. Surely it is not natural to rush, as it were, out of the presence of our hearers, so soon as we have said what was quite indispensable, without one courteous, or affectionate, farewell word. But what is more important, an invaluable opportunity is thus lost of urging home on their consciences and hearts, in a warm parting sentence, some telling inference from the theme and discourse, or telling use or application of them. Only this ought to be done briefly and unelaborately. What a pity, under the name of 'a closing word', to inflict a second and repetitory discourse on a congregation, and thus risk their wearying of the whole?

This also I am strongly persuaded of, that the 'application' – assuming there is one – ought to be regarded by the preacher as of very great importance, and the matter of it to be well considered and pre-meditated. The late distinguished Mr M'Crie, I used to hear, was accustomed to give much attention to the premeditating of his 'applications'. Certain it is that, as closing words must ever be a matter of great moment, so they deserve and demand to be earnestly and prayerfully weighed by us before the Lord.

2. PASTORAL VISITATION

After a long ministry I do not hesitate to express my belief, that if, (as has been affirmed in the Address on Preaching) the most diligent visitation of the people from house to house will be of small power without good preaching on the Sabbaths, on the other hand, the best preaching will lose much of its power without the systematic visiting of the flock at their homes.

Not only must the minister remain thus a stranger, to a large extent, to their condition and necessities, and so have to preach to them very much at random, but he shall fail of securing that kindly esteem and affectionate confidence at their hands, without which, however he may win their mere respect by his pulpit ministrations, his preaching will probably fail to a great extent of its grand use and end. As the people will most surely bid that minister right welcome to their homes whose voice they hear with joy on the Sabbaths, so will they return with fresh and ever-growing joy to the church, to listen to *his* voice whom they have found the sympathizing friend and counsellor of their loved families.

Having, however, had the benefit of a good deal of experience in the manner of conducting pastoral visitation, I will venture to offer the aid of it to my younger brethren in the ministry – only premising that, as I never was in a country charge, I can speak only to the case and care of a town congregation. When I began, then, my ministry in 1831, I used to take a very laborious method of household visitation. In order to get through the work – as I fancied, more effectually – I took what was called *a day's visiting* commencing soon after breakfast, and ending late in the afternoon. Finding usually the large Family-Bible set down for my use, I took it, and expounded a passage in every house, engaging afterwards in prayer. By degrees, this became so laborious and exhausting that I was obliged, or at least tempted, frequently to break in upon it, and soon found the visiting of the entire congregation to be a herculean task, requiring not less than two or three or four years.

At length, after following the same method for some time in my present charge, and with the like very partial success and satisfaction, it pleased God to visit me with an illness which obliged me, when I came out of it, to seek after some less laborious method of visitation. Gradually it took shape, and in the end proved so successful, that for seven consecutive years I was able, without material fatigue, to visit my whole congregation, including individual persons, such as domestic servants, in less than nine months of each year. This result came out of the following simple elements:

First, I visited only twelve families a week – six on each of two days – but *kept to this* with almost undeviating regularity.

Second, I took care to have the visits well and thoroughly arranged, and carefully intimated.

Third, I gave up the plan of formal exposition in each house. Relying on the pulpit for the more formal teaching of the flock, I now went to their houses for a different purpose – viz., to hold free spiritual intercourse with them, and, as far as possible, make their familiar acquaintance. When the large Family-Bible was now set down, I courteously expressed a preference for my own pocket one, and made use even of it quite *ad libitum* [at my own discretion] – as significant rather of the spiritual objects and ends of the visit than for regular exposition – simply taking some verse, or some incident of the time, or some circumstance in the condition of the family, on which to hang *my* part of the conversation, because it had now become an object with me to get the rest to take a share.

I never can forget what once I heard respecting the distinguished Dr Andrew Thomson, of St George's – that he used to say there was nothing more formidable to him in his ministry than when, on entering the house of some plain family of his flock for a pastoral visit, and finding the Family-Bible laid for his use, the good woman would draw

down her apron, and say, 'Noo, sir, we're a' ready.'
Well, the result of this change of method was that, in
the first place, by the simple changing of my voice to
a conversational tone, and sharing the conversation
with others (though, of course, I took the chief part),
I underwent scarcely any fatigue; and, secondly, that
I occupied not more than twenty minutes, on an
average, with each visit – praying shortly before the
close. Thus it came to pass that, finishing the whole
in about two hours and a half, I was not obliged to
begin the work before twelve, and, closing it by half-
past two, or three, had scarcely broken the backbone
of the day with it, but secured an hour or two of
home work before beginning, and left about as much
at the end, either for relaxation or more miscellane-
ous pastoral duty.

So regularly and frequently I was able thus to
return to the same house, that in place of feeling half
ashamed on leaving it – as I used to do, from the
almost hopeless interval that behoved to elapse
before the visit could be repeated – I felt, on entering
a house, as if I had seen the family but a little while
before, and thus could with the better grace make
the visit both limited in duration, and simple and
easy in character. Thus, as I have said, I continued to
visit during seven successive years, and with deep
satisfaction and joy, until my medical man forbade
regular pastoral visitation altogether.

3. COMMUNION-TABLE ADDRESSES

I have an esteemed friend in the ministry who pre-
fers dispensing the Communion without any address,
beyond the uttering of the simple words of Institu-
tion. And so far I confess I enter into the *spirit* of his
preference, that, in the first place, I would rather have
no address than an unsuitable one;[1] and, secondly,
whether there is to be a Table address or no, sufficient time ought to be allowed for the silent
intercourse of the communicants with the blessed
Lord.

No words (or, at the utmost, a well chosen word
or text of Scripture, uttered, without comment, at
short intervals) ought to be heard while the elements
are being distributed; and the time occupied in this
ought, if possible, not to be too short. Among different advantages which I have of late found to attend
simultaneous communicating, one which I highly
prize is the longer time found for silent fellowship,
and offering of intercessory, as well as personal,

---

[1] Fifty years ago a good old man, known by his Christian
friends to be somewhat deaf, was observed by one of them to
seat himself at the furthest distance from the assisting minister,
when about to address the communicants. 'John,' whispered
the friend in his ear, 'you'll not hear there.' 'I dinna' *want* to
hear', was the significant reply.

prayer.[1] On the other hand, however, I can by no means agree in opinion with my esteemed friend, and am satisfied that, for the great majority of even really Christian communicants, it is desirable to have some brief address, both before and after the distribution of the elements - provided always that, in the first place, it *be* brief, and, second, that it be in character suited to the occasion.

Now, as to this last, the simple question is, what is the true *end* of an address before the communicating? I answer – not, certainly, to examine the fitness of those at the Table for having taken their places there, nor yet to instruct them formally in the nature of the ordinance, or in anything else. Other occasions ought to have been found for all that. But the one end is, to be, if possible, somewhat *helpful to the communicants in raising their souls to fellowship with the living Lord*. And thus it follows that any address before the communicating ought neither to be of the searching nor the didactic character, but chiefly devout, meditative, contemplative, and consisting largely of words of Holy Scripture, carefully considered beforehand, and selected according to some such appropriate line of thought as perhaps

[1] If the period extend to a quarter of an hour, the last seven or eight minutes of the silence may (though I am not sure of this) be usefully broken by the simple uttering – as above hinted – of a word, or text, from Scripture, at short intervals.

the previous sermon may suggest. Earnest premeditation is a matter of the last importance, here, not only with a view to the appropriateness of the address, but that the minister may be able to avoid all such excitement and effort in speaking, as were certain to disturb the calm of spirit essential to profitable communicating.

I may be allowed to mention that in the earlier years of my ministry, I used to find Communion-table addresses the most formidable of all parts of ministerial work. In later years, by a simple attention to the things above thrown out, the difficulty has passed away, and what had been almost a positive pain has become a deep satisfaction and joy.

I know no better rule for the whole matter than this - that the minister have it for his earnest aim to meditate a few such things as, if addressed by another minister to himself when sitting at the Table, would appear likely to help his meditations, thanksgivings, lowliness of spirit, and prayerful desires, in place of disturbing and hindering them. As for the few words after the elements have been distributed, there is much less difficulty; although here also careful premeditation will be found of high importance, in order that the words may be not only few, but weighty, pointed, telling, and practical.

4. THE YOUNG, AND YOUNG COMMUNICANTS

Had I my ministry to begin anew, I should assuredly make the young a far more prominent object of both pastoral and pulpit care than, alas! I have ever done. How profound is the interest the glorious Master everywhere manifests in them! How earnest are his charges, express or implied, to care for them, 'to feed the lambs'! And how rich are all faithful labours among the young in promise of spiritual fruit!

As regards the pulpit (which I have here especially in view), surely, were we but more deeply concerned about the matter, our ordinary preaching might be somewhat more of a character which the children could profit by. Independently of occasional sermons addressed to them, might we not, by a little careful forethought, find some word in almost every discourse more expressly for the children?

I may take leave to mention that, many years ago, I was accustomed to gather all the younger part of my congregation together at the close of the afternoon service, and to go over with them the entire outline of the sermon. I was generally able to judge pretty well of the merits of my discourse from their answers. If they failed to give a tolerably good account of it (no matter what the subject might be),

I could usually trace it to some obscurity, or feebleness, or tameness, in my plan or illustrations. – But I am really half ashamed to speak of the subject of the young, bringing back, as it does, recollections of mournful and manifold shortcoming.

Then I would fain glance, finally, at the kindred subject *of dealing with young communicants*. Its momentous importance, its altogether vital place in the work of the ministry, what language shall tell? I refer to it only as regards dealing with applicants for admission to the Lord's Table, about their spiritual state. Doubtless their knowledge of divine truth, of the grand truths, more particularly, embodied in the ordinance of the Supper, is of high importance, and great care is to be taken in connection with it.

And yet might an applicant be very fit before the Lord to sit at his Table whose knowledge was but scanty; while few things are easier than for young people that have been well trained, though strangers altogether to God's grace, to give a sufficiently good account of the ordinance, and the different truths to which it relates. A miserable substitute this, truly, for a penitent, heaven-born faith, and genuine love to the Saviour!

The longer I minister I find myself the more constrained to make this last the grand subject of my private intercourse with young communicants. It is a difficult matter, no doubt, and one requiring great tenderness, affection, and prudence, as well as fidelity of dealing. But if we set ourselves to it earnestly and lovingly, no insuperable difficulty ought to stand in the way of our getting very near to the state of the applicant's soul, while making affectionate inquiry, for example, whether the state of it has ever been the occasion of real *concern*, and, if so, whether for any considerable time, or with any important results – as also respecting the motives that have prompted the desire to communicate, etc., etc.

Not that it is for us to sit in judgment on the spiritual condition of the several applicants. But then, in the first place, they can claim admission to the Lord's Table only on the footing of a profession, made in some form or other, of personal faith in the Lord Jesus, and dedication to his service.

And secondly, and apart from the mere matter of our duty as to their admission or rejection – when they come to us privately about their first communion, we have such opportunities for close and affectionate dealing with their souls as we never had before, and probably may never have again; and a deep responsibility cannot fail to rest on us for the due improvement of them.

Oh, for more, very much more, fidelity, heavenly wisdom, prayerfulness, and Christ-like affection and tenderness, in the whole of this solemn and vital matter!

I will only add that, when we cannot see our way to the admission of one or more of the applicants, it is of high importance that we do not take leave of them lightly and easily. It will often be very desirable to invite them to come to us again before the time of the first communion, lest still, peradventure, they may reach a state of mind suitable to it. But, at the least, we may not part with them without the expression of an earnest hope and expectation of seeing them again previously to the following one.

As to the communion immediately approaching, they ought to be lovingly reminded of the solemn circumstances under which they must now be spectators of it, and besought to plead with the Lord, while witnessing it, that he would make them soon his own bidden guests.

They ought further to be assured of our hearty readiness to meet with them, should they desire it, in the earlier part of the interval betwixt that and another occasion.

And finally, it is surely very manifest that, before bidding them farewell, we ought to kneel down with them, and commend them affectionately to the Lord in prayer.

THE EXPULSION FROM EDEN
– ITS CHARACTER AND LESSONS[1]

So he drove out the man (*Gen.* 3:24).

A short text, but a weighty one, forming a very material part of a chapter replete with the most solemn, awful, and yet blessed, interest to our fallen race – *So he drove out the man.* Whether is this judgment, or is it mercy? I believe that it is both judgment and mercy, and both in nearly equal degree; although the mercy will be found, indeed, wonderfully rejoicing against the judgment.

1. First, it is a word, this, of SOLEMN DIVINE JUDGMENT. 'He drove out the man.' It was a divine expulsion from the primeval paradise. In the previous verse this had been expressed in more general terms, 'The LORD God sent him forth from the garden of Eden.' Now, more specifically, he *drove*

[1] This sermon by Charles Brown is included as an example of his pulpit ministry.

him out. Nor was this divine expulsion one from the delights merely, the endlessly varied beauties and satisfactions, of that choicest part of a world which, everywhere, God had himself pronounced to be very good. It *was* this, indeed; and in this judgment of course appeared. When the man was driven forth from the paradise of earth – from all those outward, material objects which had been to him the source of far more than sinless enjoyment, since they had led him up in adoring gratitude and admiration to the glorious God – herein did the divine judgment against sin so far appear; the wrath of God was revealed from heaven against the ungodliness and unrighteousness of man.

It was as if the Lord had said, Be astonished, O ye heavens, at this, and be horribly afraid, be ye very desolate, saith the LORD; for my creature hath committed two evils: he hath forsaken me, the fountain of living waters, and hewed him out cisterns, broken cisterns, which can hold no water . . . Know, therefore, and see that it is an evil thing and bitter, that thou hast forsaken the LORD thy God, and that my fear is not in thee, saith the Lord GOD of hosts (see *Jer.* 2:12–13, 19) – *So he drove out the man.*

But there was a great deal more of judgment in the expulsion than this. Principally it was judgment, in that it was the final shutting out of the man, and in him, as we are too well assured, *of man*, our whole race fallen, from all possibility of life by the law, by the first covenant of the law. For God had entered into covenant with man. God who, apart from some such transaction, could be under no kind of obligation to his own creature, had condescended to bring himself under the obligation of a covenant, of a promise, on condition only of that obedience which is alike the duty and the privilege of the creature in all possible circumstances – a promise of everlasting life and blessedness, of which the *tree of life* in the midst of the garden was, as it were, the sacramental symbol and pledge, giving to man the happy assurance, as often as he ate of it, of the glorious, covenanted, higher, indestructible life which was to be the fruit and reward of his loyal obedience.

But man transgressed the covenant, violated the law, and, instead of the promised life, incurred the terrible death of that sentence, 'In the day thou eatest thereof, dying thou shalt die.' And now I pray you to observe the bearing of the 'driving forth of the man', as it comes out in the remarkable words of the twenty-second verse, 'And the LORD God said, Behold, the man is become as one of us' – as, at least, he hath aspired to think – 'to know good and evil:

and now, lest he put forth his hand, and take also of the tree of life' – in which no longer he hath any part – 'and eat and live for over' – as it were, and according to the original import and character of that divine pledge – 'therefore the LORD God sent him forth from the garden of Eden . . . *So he drove out the man.*' It tells of the forfeiture of the whole covenanted life. He drove the man out now even from the very symbol of the life. It was a holy, judicial expulsion from all possibility of eternal life by the first covenant, by all deeds of the law, by anything which man can himself do. The entire verse is in these words, 'So he drove out the man: and he placed at the east of the garden of Eden cherubim, and a flaming sword which turned every way, to keep the way of the tree of life.'

2. But now, if there was judgment thus, many ways, in the 'driving out of the man', there was also GLORIOUS MERCY in it – not simply notwithstanding of it, but *in* it – mercy along with the judgment, and divinely rejoicing against the judgment. To this second view of the text I am anxious a little more particularly to invite your attention.

And here the foundation of all lies in the promise of that new covenant which already, previous to the expulsion, had been revealed to man, which covenant, made properly with the eternal Son, the second Adam, the Lord from heaven, from everlasting, had been made known to our first parents immediately on the Fall, in an astonishing interview held by the Lord God with them, an interview which, on a first view of it, might seem to have been but the summoning of criminals to the bar, to receive their doom.

But on a closer examination it turns out that, while it *was* such, indeed, in one aspect of it, in another and still deeper it was glorious mercy throughout, as well as judgment, mercy strangely embedded in the very heart of judgment, and destined, in respect of all the heirs of this second covenant, everlastingly to rejoice against judgment. Into the details of the interview, however, I do not now enter. Limiting ourselves to the text, and only bearing in mind that the promise had been already given, of the seed of the woman, that should bruise the head of the serpent, and so effect a glorious victory for our fallen family over Satan, and sin with its whole fearful effects and consequences, observe now the immense, varied mercy of the 'driving out of the man'.

i. For, first, what was it but the gracious *shutting of him out from now delusive, vain, and ruinous hopes of life by the way of the law* – a thing this of the very last moment in reference to any possibility of his being saved by grace. 'He drove out the man, and placed at the east of the garden of Eden cherubim, and a flaming sword which turned every way, to keep the way of the tree of life.'

In one or other of two cases, it had, indeed, been no mercy to shut the man out from the hope of life by the law: either first, if there had still remained a possibility of life by that way; or, second, if there had been no other revealed method of life and salvation. In this latter case, better certainly to be let dream on, and somewhat pleasantly deceive and delude oneself with hope, than be awakened from sleep only to exchange dreams for hopeless despair. Or in the other case, if there had been still a possibility of life by the law, by man's own obedience to God, it had been of course no mercy to shut him out from cherishing the hope of it by that way.

But then, so very far otherwise was it, so very far from our obedience being now of the slightest avail for obtaining life, the violated law, on the contrary, consigns us to the death which is the wages of sin, as it is written, 'The law worketh wrath – By the law is the knowledge of sin – Whatsoever things the law saith, it saith to them who are under the law; that every mouth may be stopped, and all the world become guilty before God – Cursed is every one that continueth not in all things which are written in the book of the law to do them – By the deeds of the law there shall no flesh be justified in his sight – I was alive without the law once: but when the commandment came, sin revived and I died; and the commandment which was ordained to life I found to be unto death.'

Oh, so long as men cling to false and delusive hopes of life by a law which in reality condemns them to eternal death, so long as they are not *driven out* from all such hopes, in vain shall any method of life be pressed upon them, wretched, indeed, they, and miserable, and poor, and blind, and naked, but in their own eyes rich, and increased with goods, and having need of nothing.

See what mercy was in that word, 'Lest he put forth his hand and take of the tree of life . . . *so* he drove out the man.' What mercy in the shutting of him out now from even the symbol of life in the broken covenant, since the reality of life could no longer be found in connection with the symbol! Now the sign should have been but a delusive phantom; and it was just as if the Lord had said, That he may be in mercy shut out from all such ruinous hopes as the symbol might beget, I will drive him out even from the view of it – 'Therefore the LORD God sent him forth from the garden of Eden . . . he drove out the man; and he placed at the east of the garden, cherubim, and a flaming sword which turned every way, to keep the way of the tree of life.'

How often do we see men among us, let me say, utter strangers to Christ, still lying under the sentence of death in the law, yet sitting down at communion tables, only to delude themselves with the signs and symbols of life, apart altogether from the truth and reality of it! Would God they were but driven out by any means into despair of life by all obedience of their own!

Some man, whose affairs are in a state of inextricable disorder, and who must one day become bankrupt, contrives, by means of dishonourable concealments, to put off the evil day, and go on for a season, things of course growing every day worse with him. It were mercy to such a man at once to plunge him so much deeper into difficulties, that he should have no alternative but to lay his ruin open, and declare himself insolvent. What mercy, I repeat, to *the man,* was the driving of him out from all hopes of life by a covenant which now could avail only for his destruction! What mercy that flaming sword placed at the east of the garden, debarring his entrance any more where life no more was to be found, telling of wrath, indeed, but so telling graciously of it as to *shut out* from now vain and destructive hopes, on the one hand, and *shut in* to the promise of the new covenant of grace, upon the other!

ii. But thus I observe, secondly, that the driving out of the man was rich mercy, in that *it was in effect the shutting of him now also in to Christ*, the one name given under heaven among men fallen whereby we must be saved.

I have observed already that, on supposition of no other way of life having been revealed besides the law, it had been better to be let alone, and not to be driven out before the time from even delusive dreams of life. But, blessed be God, as the seed of the woman had been proclaimed before this hour to our first parents, so we are now permitted to listen to such glorious words as these: 'I am the resurrection and the life – I am the way, and the truth, and the life; no man cometh unto the Father but by me – We have seen, and do testify, that the Father sent the Son to be the Saviour of the world – I am the door; by me, if any man enter in, he shall be saved, and shall go in and out, and find pasture – The life was manifested, and we have seen it, and bear witness, and show unto you that eternal life, which was with the Father, and was manifested unto us.' What mercy to be now, even in the most terrible ways, driven forth from lying refuges, and shut up to such a Saviour, and such a salvation! 'He drove out the man', as if he had said to him in the act, No longer thou canst find life now in that first paradise; thou mayest find it, driven from it, and from all hopes of life connected with it, in him who shall bruise the head of the serpent, and open a new and living way to a yet better tree of life in the midst of the paradise of God!

Thus is it that there is not even one among all the darkest and most terrible things written in the Scriptures, which has not an aspect of richest mercy in it, as designed and fitted to drive us out of our security, our fatal slumbers, our delusive hopes, on the one hand, and to shut us in, on the other, to the Lamb of God, to him who came by water and blood, even Jesus Christ, not by water only, but by water and blood. Do you discern the flaming sword turning every way in such words as these? 'God is jealous, and the LORD revengeth; the LORD revengeth, and is furious – Their worm dieth not, and their fire is not quenched – Depart from me, ye cursed, into everlasting fire, prepared for the devil and his angels –

Mount Sinai was altogether on a smoke, because the LORD descended upon it in fire; and the smoke thereof ascended as the smoke of a furnace, and the whole mount quaked greatly.' But this sword, shutting you out from all hopes of life by the law, is but the shutting of you up and in to the faith of him who was made under the law, made a curse, who bared his bosom to the stroke of that very sword, the surety and substitute of the guilty, while the eternal Father said, 'Awake, O sword, against my shepherd, and against the man that is my fellow, saith the LORD of hosts, smite the shepherd', so that now the voice is heard, 'I am come that they might have life, and that they might have it more abundantly – Christ hath redeemed us from the curse of the law, being made a curse for us – God so loved the world, that he gave his only begotten Son, that whosoever believeth in him should not perish, but have everlasting life.'

iii. But we have not yet reached by any means the full mercy which was in the driving out of the man. So far we have seen its gracious design and tendency, more *doctrinally*, as it were, under the grace of the Holy Ghost to shut out from delusive hopes of life, and shut in to him who is the eternal life, the way, and the truth, and the life. And this truly was of unspeakable importance. How very large a portion of the Bible bears one way or other towards this double design! It might be said to be the grand scope and drift of it, doctrinally, from first to last. But then, the text opens up at least another class of *means* altogether for effecting the design.

For, practically, what is it that to a very large extent holds us back from Christ, and prevails with us to leave him and his salvation neglected and despised? Is it not some dream of finding a portion, a good, a happiness, in this world – in the lust of the flesh, or the lust of the eye, or the pride of life – for the sake of which we are prepared to run the risk of losing our never-dying souls?

But now behold the still further import of the driving out of the man. See how it was just a kind of summary, in effect, of that whole *providential discipline* which the Lord is administering from age to age in our fallen world, in connection with his Word, towards the same great end of driving us out from our vain delusive hopes of life and blessedness, on the one side, and shutting us in to the faith and love and obedience and enjoyment of the Lord Jesus Christ, upon the other.

For observe, first, what it was the Lord drove out the man *from*. It was from the paradise of earth, as from a scene now no longer suited to his state, which, however profitable as well as pleasant before, when all earthly comforts did but raise his soul in love and thankfulness to God, could now have proved but a deadly snare to him, a show of heaven without the reality of it, in all possible forms presenting to his now weakened and broken soul the very temptations to which he had at the first fallen a prey, when 'the woman saw that the tree was good for food, and that it was pleasant to the eyes, and a tree to be desired to make one wise; and she took of the fruit thereof, and did eat, and gave also to her husband with her, and he did eat.'

Hence, in rich mercy as well as judgment, 'he drove out the man', as if he should say, Outside that paradise of earth, away from its delights, now unfit for thee, thou mayest be shut in to desire a better country, even an heavenly. And just thus it is that the Lord is driving forth his children still from their Edens of earth, withering their gourds, teaching them painfully that

They build too low who build beneath the skies;

– in driving them out, only shutting them in to him who is their only life, and in whom they are yet to reach a better Eden than the primeval one.

But what, further, did God drive out the man *to*? To till the ground now by the hard toil of his hands and the sweat of his brow – 'In the sweat of thy face shalt thou eat bread, till thou return unto the ground.' And, in addition, to endure many a hardship and profound sorrow – 'Cursed is the ground for thy sake, in sorrow shalt thou eat of it all the days of thy life: thorns also and thistles shall it bring forth to thee.' And 'unto the woman he said, I will greatly multiply thy sorrow and thy conception; in sorrow thou shalt bring forth children'.

Ah, it is judgment, indeed, but at least as much mercy. 'Driven out' thus we are to a lot of toil and sorrow. But it is a lot only the more in keeping, *because* sorrowful, with our state here, as at the best sorrowfully sinful – ever ready as we are, even after having tasted that the Lord is gracious, to depart from the living God, and take up our rest here, and put some idol in the place of God, and worship the creature more than the Creator, and prefer the things which are seen and temporal to the things unseen and eternal.

How merciful the 'driving out of the man'! How wisely gracious the shutting of him up, not only more doctrinally as it were, but in all possible ways also practically and providentially, not only by the Word, but by the trials and changes and fast approaching death of this world, to lay hold of and cling to the hope set before him, to cleave with purpose of heart to the Resurrection and the Life!

What, in this last aspect of it, was the driving out of the man but the opening of that whole course of providential dealing of which we read in numberless words such as these: 'I will bring the third part through the fire, and will refine them as silver is refined, and will try them as gold is tried – Whom the Lord loveth he chasteneth, and scourgeth every son whom he receiveth – I will hedge up thy way with thorns, and will make a wall, that she shall not find her paths – I will allure her, and bring her into the wilderness, and will speak comfortably unto her – Blessed is the man whom thou chastenest, O Lord, and teachest him out of thy law – Here we have no continuing city, but we seek one to come – Refuge failed me: I cried unto thee, O Lord; I said, Thou art my refuge, and my portion in the land of the living – Although the fig-tree shall not blossom, neither shall fruit be in the vines; the labour of the olive shall fail, and the fields shall yield no meat; the flock shall be cut off from the fold, and there shall be no herd in the stalls; yet I will rejoice in the Lord, I will joy in the God of my salvation.' *So he drove out the man.*

In closing let me address a sentence or two to those among us who are still under the first broken covenant of the law, and thus necessarily under its curse, as Paul writes, 'As many as are of the works of the law are under the curse; for it is written, Cursed is every one that continueth not in all things which are written in the book of the law to do them.'

Oh, that covenant, that law, cannot save you. On the contrary, it condemns and consigns you to eternal death. It is but a sinking ship you are in. Fain you would abide in it because the idols and lusts you love are there. But soon they and you must go together to the bottom. Escape for thy life. All that a man hath will he give for his life – *this* is the life of thy never dying soul. What shall it profit thee, if thou gain the whole world, and lose thyself, thy soul?

Be content to be driven out to Christ, only too thankful to find such a refuge prepared for thee. As to trials, you must have them anyhow. No longer are we in an Eden now, whether with Christ or without him. But how terrible to miss both paradises! How fearful to have been driven out from the earthly one to the toils and trials of the wilderness, and to miss the gracious design too, miss the better country, miss Christ, and awake in the second death! Awake now, thou that sleepest, and arise from the dead, and Christ shall give thee light. Thus saith the LORD God, Behold, I lay in Zion for a foundation a stone, a tried stone, a precious corner-stone, a sure foundation; he that believeth on him shall not be confounded.

Believers on Christ, heirs of the covenant sealed in his blood, all ye that have fled for refuge to lay hold on the hope set before you, see that you live by faith, remembering what is written, 'If by grace, then it is no more of works, otherwise grace is no more grace – Ye are become dead to the law by the body of Christ, that ye should be married to another, even to him who is raised from the dead, that we should bring forth fruit unto God.'

Come up from the wilderness leaning on the Beloved. Expect no Eden upon earth. Arise and depart, for this is not your rest, it is polluted. Lay your account with trials and afflictions. See judgment, sin, in them. But see also rich mercy. Say with David, I will sing of mercy and of judgment. It is good for me that I have been afflicted, that I might learn thy statutes. And anticipate the holy, everlasting blessedness of which it is written, 'He showed me a pure river of water of life, clear as crystal, proceeding out of the throne of God and of the Lamb. In the midst of the street of it, and on either side of the river, was there the tree of life . . . And there shall be no more curse: but the throne of God and of the Lamb shall be in it; and his servants shall serve him; and they shall see his face; and his name shall be in their foreheads.'